An Approach to Shakespeare

An Approach
to Shakespeare

Gilian West

CASSELL

Cassell
Wellington House
125 Strand
London WC2R 0BB

215 Park Avenue South
New York
NY 10003

The extracts from Shakespeare's plays in this book have been taken with permission from the Collins Classics Alexander text of the Complete Works of Shakespeare © 1994.

British Library Cataloguing-in-Publication Data
A catalogue record for this book is available from the British Library.

Library of Congress Cataloging-in-Publication Data
West, Gilian.
    An approach to Shakespeare / Gilian West.
        p.   cm. — (Cassell education)
    ISBN 0-304-33098-1 (pbk.): $26.00
    1. Shakespeare, William, 1564–1616—Study and teaching.
    2. English drama—Study and teaching.   I. Title.   II. Series.
PR2987.W47   1995
822.3'3—dc20   94–41562
                                                          CIP

ISBN 0–304–33098–1

Typeset by York House Typographic Ltd, London
Printed and bound in Great Britain by Redwood Books, Trowbridge, Wiltshire

Contents

Contents

Preface

This is a textbook with a dual purpose. It seeks to provide for young people an enjoyable means of becoming familiar with Shakespeare's language, style and dramatic methods. At the same time it exploits Shakespeare (who better?) as a source of 'knowledge about language'.

THE TEXTBOOK AS A SHAKESPEARE COURSE

Every teacher wants the young people in his or her charge to enjoy Shakespeare, not just in school, but throughout the rest of their lives. The National Curriculum urges secondary school teachers to make the attempt to introduce his work into the classroom: 'every pupil should be given at least some experience of the plays or poetry of Shakespeare', as the Cox Report says (DES, 1989, para. 7.15).

A great deal is being asked here of the English teacher. Shakespeare can present extreme difficulty in the contemporary classroom. Young people, confronted with a language which they are told is their own but which may well seem to them entirely foreign, can feel angry or humiliated. They are expected to feel awe for a writer who cannot even write understandable English.

The Cox Report perhaps recognizes this when it continues:

> Whether this [experience] is through the study, viewing or performance of whole plays or of selected poems or scenes should be entirely at the discretion of the teacher. (*Ibid.*, para. 7.15)

This book is for those teachers who feel that their students are not yet at a stage in their linguistic and literary development where they are ready to tackle the text of a whole play. I hope it provides a preliminary training that will give such students not only the ability but also the *active desire* to study, or to go to the theatre to see, a whole play.

The Cox Report's suggestion for selecting scenes sets the teacher an impossible task. Scenes have to be found that:

are involving and dramatic;
have a self-explanatory action;
have characters whose motives are apparent;
are free of irrecoverable lines or textual problems;

are not from the later plays where the style is – let us be honest for once – *extremely* tortuous;

can be read or performed to an audience.

Of course there are no such scenes in Shakespeare. To create scripts for the classroom that are both dramatic and intelligible in isolation, I have found few scenes to choose from, and these have had to be pruned of unnecessary obscurities and extraneous characters and patched here and there to conceal omissions. I hope no reader will feel that this pruning has done violence to the text. At least I have not bowdlerized it.

The Cox Report also advises that 'the once-traditional method where desk-bound pupils read the text' should be replaced by 'exciting, enjoyable approaches that are social, imaginative and physical' (para 7.16). It recommends a 'participatory, exploratory approach', making Shakespeare 'accessible, meaningful and enjoyable'.

The extracts, and sequences of extracts, collected here are followed by questions and suggestions for projects which I hope will help the teacher to pursue such ideals.

There are questions on moral and social issues (e.g., can we pity a serial killer? how have attitudes to marriage changed? can honour be over-valued?). Other questions encourage students to put themselves in the dramatist's place, in order to increase their pleasure in his artistry. Others urge students to make use of what they have learned from Shakespeare about language and drama in creative writing – poetry, narrative and dialogue – of their own. This work, however personally beneficial, would not be entirely an end in itself:

> Learning about the construction of an effective text is much better done ... through writing than through critical analysis . . . . The understanding of craft and construction that develops through writing leads to a more realistic appreciation of the achievements of literary authors.
> (*Teaching through Poetry*, George Marsh, 1988, p.23, quoted in the Cox Report, para. 7.9.)

Students are also asked to exercise their theatrical imaginations in interpreting Shakespeare's drama for an audience, and the final question at the end of the last sequence suggests that they might, borrowing some of Shakespeare's techniques, collaborate in creating a drama of their own on a topical issue.

The book contains scenes of romance and battle, slapstick and horror. No one who reads it will ever claim that Shakespeare is dull. The course will prove to students that he is as intensely concerned as they are with greed, guilt, ambition, loyalty and every other aspect of human nature.

Part One contains nine scripts taken from various plays (a few lines of introduction supply the context), and one poem. There is no need to know anything whatever about the source-play in order to enjoy the extract.

Part Two contains six short extracts from *The Comedy of Errors*, linked by brief narrative explanation, so that they create a condensation of the whole play's action.

Part Three contains ten extracts from Shakespeare's early history plays. They are in chronological order and linked by brief narrative explanations. Together they form an independent drama, which can be appreciated without any further knowledge of the Histories.

THE TEXTBOOK AS AN ENGLISH LANGUAGE COURSE

The Kingman Report (DES, 1988) gives us many reasons why students must read the great literature of the past; among others, these:

> to acquire sensitivity to the use of language (i.e. to acquire 'an ear for language', p.11);

> to improve their own use of language (reading the literature of the past is 'a *reception* of language' which 'allows the individual greater possibilities of *production* of language', p.11);

> to learn about the *history* of the language, (because such knowledge is of enormous benefit in developing 'an awareness and understanding of changes in the language which are taking place in our time', p.36);

> to appreciate *modern* writing ('Our modern language and our modern writing have grown out of the language and literature of the past. The rhythms of our daily speech and writing are haunted ... by the rhythms of Shakespeare, Blake, Edward Lear, Lewis Carroll, the Authorized Version of the Bible. We do not completely know what modern writing is unless we know what lies behind it.', p.11).

These extracts from Shakespeare are a mine of information about the history of English, about its varieties, both written and spoken, and about devices of literary style. The class may plunder it at will, but to stimulate and encourage such plundering, the questions following the extracts direct attention to linguistic and stylistic detail.

The Cox Report insists that students must be helped to develop their abilities not merely in writing English, but also in describing and criticizing its use; in speaking; and in listening. The questions are designed to promote all these skills.

Students are asked to consider why the language of the extracts is so different from the colloquial language of today; how language is made forceful or poignant; how language can be manipulated to achieve wit; how language is adapted according to genre, mood, register and personality.

Students will grow accustomed to questioning whether a word is being used in its familiar sense, and will become keenly aware that words are constantly changed in meaning, or replaced. While archaisms that would seriously impede understanding are glossed, the meaning of others must be deduced from the context. Teachers will no doubt encourage the use of a dictionary, preferably an historical dictionary, to confirm such deductions. Students will also acquire the habit of looking for unusual grammar, inversions of word-order, idioms, oaths and terms of address. Thus the course should instil in them the knowledge that English is not the preserve of any one era or society, fixed and correct, but a living organism infinitely adaptable to circumstance.

Some questions requiring argument on abstract issues or empathetic defence of a character's case should stimulate the kind of debate, formal or informal in organization, in which students develop their oral and aural skills. Other questions encourage students to experiment with literary techniques in prose and poetry.

In performing, or visualizing a performance of, the scenes, students should gain insight into the importance and variety of non-verbal methods of communication.

WHY ARE MANY OF THE EXTRACTS TAKEN FROM SHAKESPEARE'S EARLY PLAYS?

Shakespeare's early plays are especially suited to the purposes of this book. There his language is governed by the Elizabethan fashion for Ciceronian rhetoric. Although it is far enough removed from our everyday experience to present a challenge, it is also logical, clearly ordered and organized. His Elizabethan style is being used to prepare students to cope with his Jacobean style.

Young people working together on these scenes from his early comedies can indulge themselves in Shakespeare at his most hilarious; those who become involved in the relentless ironies of his early histories will never forget the experience. There they will be forced to confront the evil in humanity; there they will witness scenes of depravity and grief as dreadful as any we see in today's news reports.

WHY IS THE METRE MARKED IN?

In verse scenes I have marked in the metre – as best I may, for there is no certainty in this matter – to provide a rough guide for students who are not used to reading verse aloud. There is at present a general neglect of the structure of Shakespeare's verse in schools and in the theatre. For justification of my strategy I turn to one theatre director who believes fervently that it is *essential* to understand the metre: Sir Peter Hall. Actors who have a trained awareness of the metre, he claims, will hold the audience's attention and help them both to follow the sense and to feel the emotion of the verse.

Tirzah Lowen (1990, pp. 27–9) quotes Sir Peter talking to his actors at a rehearsal:

> 'Find the beat, the ongoing rhythm; then you can do anything ... I beg you, don't see this as a frightful imprisonment: it's the very opposite, it frees you, and the new discipline will add to your strength.
>
> '... every single line in Shakespeare will scan. Your business is to find and keep as close to the five beats of the iambic pentameter as possible and then decide on what's right for you in terms of emphasis and colour .... By modernizing, not keeping to the beat, we hold the verse up, make it slower, and the play loses its tension – and its hold on our attention.'

The actors present at this rehearsal agree 'that both the sense of a line and its emotional content are clearly indicated once they find the pulse of the metre'.

The author watches Judi Dench rehearse: 'Her handling of the scansion by now innate ("You work at it, work at it and suddenly it becomes a part of you which you never lose"), she has the freedom and confidence to experiment, using the verse as a springboard.'

Tim Piggott-Smith is enthusiastic: 'The language is marvellous. By following the scansion, you find the sense and the emotion works for itself. You don't have to pump it out.'

Anthony Hopkins tells the author that he finds Hall's approach to the verse 'immensely exciting and enabling; there is an almost physical relish of the language, a pleasure in mastering its shape and colouring.'

REFERENCES

Department of Education and Science (1988) *Report of the Committee of Inquiry into the Teaching of English Language* (The Kingman Report). HMSO: London.

Department of Education and Science and the Welsh Office (1989) *English for Ages 5 to 16* (The Cox Report). HMSO: London.

Tirzah Lowen (1990) *Peter Hall Directs 'Antony and Cleopatra'*. Methuen: London.

A Note on Shakespeare's Verse

When Shakespeare writes in verse-form most of his lines have ten syllables and he chooses and arranges his words so that the reader can give heavier stress to every second syllable:

This níght you sháll behóld him át our féast.

Many of his lines, however, do not conform precisely to this pattern, and, when they don't, this is usually because, perhaps for extra dramatic emphasis, he has chosen *either* to begin the line with a heavy stress:

Jústice, sweet Prínce, agáinst that wóman thére!

or to begin a second part of the line with a heavy stress:

Or, wíth the rést, /whére is your dárling Rútland?

You will notice from one of the examples quoted above that his lines may also be irregular in that they have an extra, eleventh, syllable after the fifth stress.

By marking what seem to me the more heavily stressed syllables in the verse, I have tried to give the newcomer to Shakespeare an idea of the pattern governing his choice of phrase. In performing the text actors have the difficult task of trying to sound as natural as they can without forgetting that they are not speaking prose.

Part One

Autolycus and the Shepherd

The scene is a country road. Autolycus, a ragged pedlar, meets a young shepherd on his way to market.

[*Enter Autolycus, singing*]

AUTOLYCUS   When daffodils begin to peer,
　　　With heigh! the <u>doxy</u> over the dale　　　　　　　　　　　[*girl*
Why, then comes in the sweet o' the year,
　　　For the red blood reigns in the winter's pale.

A prize! a prize!

[*Enter Shepherd*]

SHEPHERD   [*To himself*]   Let me see: what am I to buy for our sheep-shearing feast? Three pound of sugar, five pound of currants, rice – what will this sister of mine do with rice? But my father hath made her mistress of the feast, and she lays it on. I must have saffron to colour the <u>warden</u>　　　[*a kind of pear* pies; mace; dates – none, that's out of my note; nutmegs, seven; a <u>race</u> or two of ginger, but that I may beg; four pounds of　　　[*root* prunes, and as many of raisins o' th' sun.

AUTOLYCUS   [*Grovelling on the ground*]   O that ever I was born!

SHEPHERD   I' th' name of me!

AUTOLYCUS   O, help me, help me! Pluck but off these rags; and then death, death!

SHEPHERD   Alack, poor soul! thou hast need of more rags to lay on thee, rather than have these off.

AUTOLYCUS   O sir, the loathsomeness of them offend me more than the stripes I have received, which are mighty ones and millions.

SHEPHERD   Alas, poor man! a million of beating may come to a great matter.

AUTOLYCUS   I am robb'd, sir, and beaten; my money and apparel ta'en from me, and these detestable things put upon me.

SHEPHERD   Lend my thy hand, I'll help thee. Come, lend me thy hand.
[*Helping him up*]

AUTOLYCUS   O, good sir, tenderly, O!

3

SHEPHERD	Alas, poor soul!
AUTOLYCUS	O, good sir, softly, good sir; I fear, sir, my shoulder blade is out.
SHEPHERD	How now? Canst stand?
AUTOLYCUS	Softly, dear sir. [*Picks his pocket*] Good sir, softly. You ha' done me a charitable office.
SHEPHERD	Dost lack any money? I have a little money for thee.
AUTOLYCUS	No, good sweet sir; no, I beseech you, sir. I have a kinsman not past three-quarters of a mile hence, unto whom I was going; I shall there have money or anything I want. Offer me no money, I pray you; that kills my heart.
SHEPHERD	How do you now?
AUTOLYCUS	Sweet sir, much better than I was; I can stand and walk. I will even take my leave of you and pace softly towards my kinsman's.
SHEPHERD	Shall I bring thee on the way?
AUTOLYCUS	No, good-fac'd sir; no, sweet sir.
SHEPHERD	Then fare thee well. I must go buy spices for our sheep-shearing.
AUTOLYCUS	Prosper you, sweet sir!

[*Exit Shepherd*]

Your purse is not hot enough to purchase your spice.

Jog on, jog on, the footpath way
   And merrily <u>hent</u> the stile-a;   [*seize*
A merry heart goes all the day,
   Your sad tires in a mile-a.

[*Exit*]

[from *The Winter's Tale*, Act IV, Scene i]

Questions

1. What in Autolycus's speeches suggests that he is pretending to be a grand gentleman?

2. In Shakespeare's time it was possible to address another person as either 'you' or 'thou'. Judging from this scene, which do you think was the more formal term?

3. Which two remarks of Autolycus's are to be taken in more than one sense?

4. Which Bible story does this episode remind you of? Would Shakespeare want us to notice the similarity?

5. Why does Autolycus refuse the Shepherd's offer of money?

6. What could the actors do to win the audience's sympathy or admiration for (i) the pedlar or (ii) the Shepherd?

7. Why does Shakespeare give Autolycus a song at the beginning and end of the scene?

8. Write the dialogue for a scene between the Shepherd and his sister when he gets home without her groceries. Do you think she *ought* to be angry with him? Imagine his sister as you wish, but try to keep to Shakespeare's characterization of the Shepherd.

Lady Macbeth

The year is 1057, and the scene Macbeth's castle in Scotland, at night. Macbeth, encouraged and aided by his wife, has murdered the King of Scotland and seized the crown. Lady Macbeth has seemed more ruthless than her husband.

[*Enter a Doctor and a Lady-in-waiting*]

DOCTOR	I have two nights watch'd with you, but can perceive no truth in your report. When was it she last walk'd?
LADY	Since his Majesty went into the field, I have seen her rise from her bed, throw her nightgown upon her, unlock her closet, take forth paper, fold it, write upon't, read it, afterwards seal it, and again return to bed; yet all this while in a most fast sleep.
DOCTOR	What, at any time, have you heard her say?
LADY	That, sir, which I will not report after her.
DOCTOR	You may to me.
LADY	Neither to you nor any one, having no witness to confirm my speech.

[*Enter Lady Macbeth, with a candle*]

	Lo you, here she comes! and, upon my life, fast asleep. Observe her; stand close.
DOCTOR	How came she by that light?
LADY	Why, it stood by her. She has light by her continually; 'tis her command.
DOCTOR	You see, her eyes are open.
LADY	Ay, but their sense is shut.
DOCTOR	What is it she does now? Look how she rubs her hands.
LADY	It is an accustomed action with her, to seem thus washing her hands; I have known her continue in this a quarter of an hour.
LADY MACBETH	Yet here's a spot.
DOCTOR	Hark, she speaks. I will set down what comes from her, to satisfy my remembrance the more strongly.

LADY MACBETH	Out, damned spot! out, I say! One, two; why then 'tis time to do't. Hell is murky. Fie, my lord, fie! a soldier, and afeard? What need we fear who knows it, when none can call our pow'r to account? Yet who would have thought the old man to have had so much blood in him?
DOCTOR	Do you mark that?
LADY MACBETH	What, will these hands ne'er be clean? No more o' that, my lord, no more o' that; you mar all with this starting.
DOCTOR	Go to, go to; you have known what you should not.
LADY	She has spoke what she should not, I am sure of that. Heaven knows what she has known.
LADY MACBETH	Here's the smell of the blood still. All the perfumes of Arabia will not sweeten this little hand. Oh, oh, oh!
DOCTOR	What a sigh is there! The heart is sorely <u>charg'd</u>. [*overburdened*
LADY	I would not have such a heart in my bosom for the dignity of the whole body.
DOCTOR	Well, well, well.
LADY	Pray God it be, sir.
DOCTOR	This disease is beyond my practice. Yet I have known those which have walk'd in their sleep who have died holily in their beds.
LADY MACBETH	Wash your hands, put on your nightgown, look not so pale. To bed, to bed; there's knocking at the gate. Come, come, come, come, give me your hand. What's done cannot be undone. To bed, to bed, to bed.

[*Exit*]

DOCTOR	Will she go now to bed?
LADY	Directly.
DOCTOR	Foul whísp'rings áre abróad. Unnátural déeds Do bréed unnátural tróubles; infécted mínds To théir deaf píllows wíll dischárge their sécrets. More néeds she thé <u>divíne</u> than thé physícian. [*priest* God, Gód forgíve us áll. Look áfter hér; Remóve from hér the méans of áll annóyance, And stíll keep éyes upón her. Só, good níght. My mínd she has <u>máted</u>, ánd amáz'd my síght. [*bewildered* I thínk, but dáre not spéak.
LADY	Good níght, good dóctor.

[*Exeunt*]

[from *Macbeth*, Act V, Scene i]

Questions

1. Would you say that before Lady Macbeth appears the Doctor and the Lady are chatting casually? Examine the language closely before you answer.

2. What does Lady Macbeth give away about the murder of the king?

3. Perhaps to add to the strangeness of the scene, Shakespeare has chosen to use some very unnatural language here, where much meaning is compressed into few words. Can you explain:

    (a) to satisfy my remembrance the more strongly

    (b)   infected minds
        To their deaf pillows will discharge their secrets.

    (c) Remove from her the means of all annoyance.

4. Could we not have watched Lady Macbeth walking in her sleep for ourselves? How does the commentary of the Doctor and the Lady-in-waiting affect our reactions?

5. Contrast the language of Lady Macbeth here with that of the Doctor, especially in his speech at the close of the scene. Does she sound like a Queen? Does he sound like a Doctor?

6. Apart from the words glossed, which other expressions do we no longer use? Suggest what they mean. Why has the meaning of 'abroad' changed?

7. If you were to translate the following phrases into modern English, how would you re-form the verbs?
    How came she by that light?
    look not so pale
    Hark, she speaks.

8. When life turns out to be not at all as we expected, we call the surprise 'ironic'. Explain the ironies behind some of the remarks in this scene, and consider especially 'none can call our pow'r to account'.

9. What kind of décor, lighting and sound would you choose to increase the emotional effect of this scene, if you were staging it?

Juliet

In Verona, the Capulet household is preparing for a feast. Lady Capulet comes to tell her daughter, Juliet, that among the guests will be a young gentleman, Paris, who wishes to marry her. As it chances, this same night Juliet will meet Romeo.

[*Enter Lady Capulet and Nurse*]

LADY CAPULET	Nurse, whére's my dáughter? Cáll her fórth to mé.
NURSE	What, lámb! what, lády-bírd!
	Gód forbid! Whére's this gírl? What, Júliét!

[*Enter Juliet*]

JULIET	How now, who calls?
NURSE	Your mother.
JULIET	Mádam, I am hére. What ís your wíll?
LADY CAPULET	Thís is the mátter. Núrse, give léave awhíle,
	We must tálk in sécret. Núrse, come báck agáin;
	I háve remémber'd mé, thou's héar our cóunsel.
	Thou knówest my dáughter's óf a prétty áge.
NURSE	Faith, Í can téll her áge untó an hóur.
LADY CAPULET	She's nót fourtéen.
NURSE	I'll láy fourtéen of my téeth –
	And yét, to my <u>téen</u> be it spóken, I háve but fóur –
	She's nót fourtéen. Hów long ís it nów
	To Lámmas-tíde?
LADY CAPULET	A fórtnight ánd odd dáys.
NURSE	Éven or ódd, of áll days ín the yéar,
	Come Lámmas Éve at níght shall she bé fourtéen.
	Súsan and shé – God rést all Chrístian sóuls! –
	Were óf an áge. Well, Súsan ís with Gód;
	She wás too góod for mé. But, ás I sáid,
	On Lámmas Éve at níght shall she bé fourtéen;

[grief

NURSE *(continued)*	That sháll she, <u>márry</u>; Í remémber it wéll.	[*an oath*
	'Tis sínce the éarthquake nów eléven yéars;	
	And thén she could stánd high-lóne; náy, <u>by th'róod</u>,	[*an oath*
	She cóuld have rún and wáddled áll abóut;	
	For éven the dáy befóre, she bróke her brów;	
	And thén my húsband – Gód be wíth his sóul!	
	'A wás a mérry mán – took úp the chíld.	
	'Yéa', quoth he 'dóst thou fáll upón thy fáce?	
	Thou wílt fall báckward whén thou hást more wít,	
	Wílt thou not, Júle?' And, <u>bý my hólidám</u>,	[*an oath*
	The prétty wrétch left crýing, ánd said 'Áy'.	
	To sée, now, hów a jést shall cóme abóut!	
	I wárrant, an Í should líve a thóusand yéars,	
	I néver shóuld forgét it: 'Wílt thou not, Júle?' quoth hé;	
	And, prétty fóol, it <u>stínted</u>, ánd said 'Áy'.	[*stopped*
LADY CAPULET	Enóugh of thís; I práy thee hóld thy péace.	
NURSE	Yes, mádam. Yét I cánnot chóose but láugh	
	To thínk it shóuld leave crýing ánd say 'Áy'.	
	And yét, I wárrant, it hád upón <u>it</u> brów	[*its*
	A búmp as bíg ás a young cóck'rel's <u>stóne</u> –	[*testicle*
	A périlous knóck; ánd it cried bítterlý.	
	'Yéa', quoth my húsband 'fáll'st upón thy fáce?	
	Thou wílt fall báckward whén thou cómest to áge;	
	Wílt thou not, Júle?' it <u>stínted</u>, ánd said 'Áy'.	[*stopped*
JULIET	And stínt thou tóo, I práy thee, núrse, say Í.	
NURSE	Peace, Í have dóne. God márk thee tó his gráce!	
	Thou wást the préttiest bábe that é'er I núrs'd;	
	An Í might líve to sée thee márried ónce,	
	I háve my wísh.	
LADY CAPULET	Márry, that 'márry' ís the véry théme	
	I cáme to tálk of. Téll me, dáughter Júliet,	
	How stánds your dispositíons tó be márried?	
JULIET	It ís an hónour thát I dréam not óf.	
LADY CAPULET	Well, thínk of márriage nów. Yóunger than yóu,	
	Hére in Veróna, ládies óf estéem,	
	Are máde alréady móthers. Bý my cóunt,	
	I wás your móther múch upón these yéars	
	That yóu are nów a máid. Thus, thén, in bríef:	
	The váliant Páris séeks you fór his lóve.	

NURSE	A mán, young lády! lády, súch a mán As áll the wórld – why, hé's a mán of wáx.
LADY CAPULET	Veróna's súmmer háth not súch a flówer.
NURSE	Nay, hé's a flówer; in fáith, a véry flówer.
LADY CAPULET	What sáy you? Cán you lóve the géntlemán? This níght you sháll behóld him át our féast; Speak bríefly, cán you líke of Páris' lóve?
JULIET	I'll lóok to líke, if lóoking líking móve.

[*Enter a Servant*]

SERVANT	Madam, the guests are come, supper serv'd up, you call'd, my young lady ask'd for, the nurse curs'd in the pantry, and everything in extremity. I must hence to wait; I beseech you, follow straight.
LADY CAPULET	We follow thee.

[*Exeunt*]

[from *Romeo and Juliet*, Act I, Scene iii]

Questions

1. By studying the use of 'you' and 'thou' in this scene, what can you learn about the relationships between the characters?

2. What is it about the Nurse's language that makes us laugh? Is she a very religious person?

3. If you were to translate the following clauses into modern English, how would you re-form the verbs?

   > Who calls?
   >
   > What say you?
   >
   > Verona's summer hath not such a flower.

4. Both Juliet and her mother have to ask the Nurse to stop talking, but they do not use 'please' to make the request sound polite. What *do* they use?

5. The Nurse uses 'ay' and 'nay'. Does anyone still use these words today?

6. What do you suppose Lady Capulet might mean when she says 'my daughter's of a pretty age'? Do you agree with the attitudes towards marriage expressed here?

7. Juliet says little in this scene. How could the actress playing the part show the audience her feelings towards her mother and the nurse, and towards the prospect of marrying?

8. Why do you think the servant's speech is written in prose rather than verse?

The Death of Talbot

The year is 1453 and the scene is a field of battle near Bordeaux. A small force of English soldiers find themselves hemmed in on all sides by French armies. There is no hope of rescue. In this desperate situation, their commander, Lord Talbot, is joined by his young son.

[*Enter Talbot and John, his son*]

TALBOT
O yóung John Tálbot! Í did sénd for thée
To tútor thée in strátagéms of wár,
That Tálbot's náme might bé in thée revív'd
When sápless áge and wéak unáble límbs
Should bríng thy fáther tó his dróoping cháir.
But – Ó malígnant ánd ill-bóding stárs! –
Now thóu art cóme untó a féast of déath,
A térriblé and únavóided dánger;
Therefóre, dear bóy, móunt on my swíftest hórse,
And Í'll diréct thee hów thou shált escápe
By súdden flíght. Come, dálly nót, be góne.

JOHN
Is mý name Tálbot, ánd am Í your són?
And sháll I flý? O, íf you lóve my móther,
Dishónour nót her hónouráble náme,
To máke a bástard ánd a sláve of mé!
The wórld will sáy he ís not Tálbot's blóod
That básely fléd when nóble Tálbot stóod.

TALBOT
Flý to revénge my déath, if Í be sláin.

JOHN
Hé that flies só will né'er retúrn agáin.

TALBOT
If wé both stáy, we bóth are súre to díe.

JOHN	Then lét me stáy; and, fáther, dó you flý.
	Your lóss is gréat, só your regárd should bé;
	My wórth unknówn, no lóss is knówn in mé;
	Upón my déath the Frénch can líttle bóast;
	In yóurs they wíll, in yóu all hópes are lóst.
	Flíght cannot stáin the hónour yóu have wón;
	But míne it wíll, that nó explóit have dóne;
	You fléd for vántage, évery óne will swéar;
	But íf I bów, they'll sáy it wás for féar.
	There ís no hópe that éver Í will stáy
	Íf the first hóur I shrínk and rún awáy.
	Hére, on my knée, I bég mortálitý,
	Ráther than lífe presérv'd with ínfamý.
TALBOT	Shall áll thy móther's hópes líe in one tómb?
JOHN	Áy, rather thán I'll sháme my móther's wómb.
TALBOT	Upón my bléssing, Í commánd thee gó.
JOHN	To fíght I wíll, but nót to flý the fóe.
TALBOT	Párt of thy fáther máy be sáv'd in thée.
JOHN	No párt of hím but wíll be sháme in mé.
TALBOT	Thou néver hádst renówn, nor cánst not lóse it.
JOHN	Yes, yóur renównëd náme; shall flíght abúse it?
TALBOT	Thy fáther's chárge shall cléar thee fróm that stáin.
JOHN	You cánnot wítness fór me, béing sláin.
	If déath be só appárent, thén both flý.
TALBOT	And léave my fóllowers hére to fíght and díe?
	My áge was néver táinted wíth such sháme.
JOHN	And sháll my yóuth be guílty óf such bláme?
	No móre can Í be sévered fróm your síde
	Than cán yoursélf yoursélf in twáin divíde.
	Stay, gó, do whát you wíll, the líke do Í;
	For líve I wíll not íf my fáther díe.
TALBOT	Then hére I táke my léave of thée, fair són,
	Bórn to eclípse thy lífe this áfternóon.
	Come, síde by síde togéther líve and díe;
	And sóul with sóul from Fránce to héaven flý.

[*Exeunt. Alarum; excursions. Enter Talbot, led by a Servant*]

TALBOT	Whére is my óther lífe? Mine ówn is góne.
	O, whére's young Tálbot? Whére is váliant Jóhn?

[*Enter Soldiers, bearing the body of John*]

SERVANT O mý dear lórd, lo whére your són is bórne!

TALBOT O thóu whose wóunds becóme <u>hard-fávour'd</u> Déath,   [*hard-featured*

Spéak to thy fáther ére thou yíeld thy bréath!

<u>Brave</u> Déath by spéaking, whéther he wíll or nó;   [*defy*

Imágine hím a Frénchman ánd thy fóe.

Poor bóy! he smíles, methínks, as whó should sáy,

Had Déath been Frénch, then Déath had díed to-dáy.

Come, cóme, and láy him ín his fáther's árms.

My spírit cán no lónger béar these hárms.

Sóldiers, adíeu! I háve what Í would háve,

Now mý old árms are yóung John Tálbot's gráve.

[*Dies*]

[from *Henry VI, Part One*, Act IV, Scenes v and vi]

Questions

1. In the following lines:

    > When sapless age and weak unable limbs
    > Should bring thy father to his drooping chair

    explain the phrases 'sapless age' and 'his drooping chair'.

2. Did you notice Talbot's use of a (very common) pun?

3. Two of many 'rhetorical' devices (i.e. devices for elevating the style) used in this scene are the rhetorical question (a question that does not require an answer) and the paradox (a statement that conflicts with what seems reasonable or possible). How do these two devices heighten the emotional power of the scene?

4. 'if I be slain'
    'if Death be so apparent'
    What have these two clauses in common that causes Shakespeare to use 'be' rather than 'am' or 'is'?

5. Most of this scene is written in 'rhyming couplets', that is, in pairs of lines. Suggest why Shakespeare *shares* the couplets between the two speakers in the middle of the scene.

6. Compose a short speech, imitating if you like the verse in this scene, either for Lady Talbot when news is brought to her of the tragedy, or for an old soldier reminiscing about the battle.

7. Do you think John was right to stay? Could his father have used any other arguments to persuade him to leave? Where does Talbot put the blame for the tragedy?

8. A performance of this scene would, of course, be more exciting if some part of the battle could be seen. Describe the fighting you would stage to demonstrate John's courage and to justify his father's pride in him. To make your performance look authentic, find out what you can about the style of warfare in 1453.

The Watch

Dogberry, the Town Constable, is proud of his office and confident of his fitness to hold it. One of his duties is to send watchmen patrolling the streets through the night, and here – with help from his friend Verges – he is giving the men their instructions. We shall find, however, that he has some very strange ideas of 'what belongs to a watch'!

[*Enter Dogberry, Verges and Watchmen*]

VERGES	Well, give them their charge, neighbour Dogberry.
DOGBERRY	First, who think you the most desartless man to be constable?
IST WATCHMAN	Hugh Oatcake, sir, or George Seacoal; for they can write and read.
DOGBERRY	Come hither, neighbour Seacoal. You are thought here to be the most senseless and fit man for the constable of the watch; therefore bear you the lantern. This is your charge: you shall comprehend all <u>vagrom</u> men; you are to bid any man stand, in the Prince's name. [*vagrants, beggars*
2ND WATCHMAN	How if 'a will not stand?
DOGBERRY	Why, then, take no note of him, but let him go; and presently call the rest of the watch together, and thank God you are rid of a <u>knave</u>. [*villain*
VERGES	If he will not stand when he is bidden, he is none of the Prince's subjects.
DOGBERRY	True, and they are to meddle with none but the Prince's subjects. You shall also make no noise in the streets; for for a watch to babble and to talk is most tolerable and not to be endured.
2ND WATCHMAN	We will rather sleep than talk; we know what belongs to a watch.
DOGBERRY	Why, you speak like an ancient and most quiet watchman, for I cannot see how sleeping should offend; only, have a care that your <u>bills</u> be not stol'n. Well, you are to call at all the ale-houses, and bid those that are drunk get them to bed. [*spears*
2ND WATCHMAN	How if they will not?

DOGBERRY	Why, then, let them alone till they are sober; if they make you not then the better answer, you may say they are not the men you took them for.
2ND WATCHMAN	Well, sir.
DOGBERRY	If you meet a thief, you may suspect him, by virtue of your office, to be no true man; and, for such kind of men, the less you meddle or make with them, why, the more is for your honesty.
2ND WATCHMAN	If we know him to be a thief, shall we not lay hands on him?
DOGBERRY	Truly, by your office you may, but I think they that touch pitch will be defil'd; the most peaceable way for you, if you do take a thief, is to let him show himself what he is, and steal out of your company.
VERGES	You have been always called a merciful man, partner.
DOGBERRY	Truly, I would not hang a dog by my will, much more a man who hath any honesty in him.
VERGES	If you hear a child cry in the night, you must call to the nurse and bid her still it.
2ND WATCHMAN	How if the nurse be asleep and will not hear us?
DOGBERRY	Why, then, depart in peace, and let the child wake her with crying. This is the end of the charge: you, constable, are to present the Prince's own person; if you meet the Prince in the night, you may stay him.
VERGES	Nay, by'r lady, that I think 'a cannot.
DOGBERRY	Five shillings to one on't, with any man that knows the statues, he may stay him; marry, not without the Prince be willing; for, indeed, the watch ought to offend no man, and it is an offence to stay a man against his will.
VERGES	By'r lady, I think it be so.
DOGBERRY	Ha, ah, ha! Well, masters, good night; an there be any matter of weight chances, call up me; keep your fellows' counsels and your own, and good night. Come, neighbour.
2ND WATCHMAN	Well, masters, we hear our charge; let us go sit here upon the church bench till two, and then all to bed.

[*Exeunt*]

[from *Much Ado about Nothing*, Act III, Scene iii]

Questions

1. Where does Dogberry go wrong in his interpretation of the watchmen's duties? Is he 'a merciful man'?

2. What is so odd about Dogberry's vocabulary? Where is his best effort at wit?

3. 'Presently' as used here means 'immediately'. Can you suggest why its meaning has changed?
   Why do we no longer use the word 'shillings'?
   Why do we no longer use the word 'master' as a term of address?
   Explain why the use of 'stay' in this scene seems strange to us.

4. In the sentence that begins 'an there be any matter of weight chances . . . ', what does 'an' mean? Do we still use 'for' (as in 'for, indeed, the watch ought to offend no man') in spoken and written language?

5. If you were playing the Second Watchman, what sort of character would you give him?

6. Does your Dictionary of Quotations tell you the source of 'they that touch pitch will be defil'd'?

7. Have you seen any other comedy – in films, perhaps, or on television – where police officers or soldiers are made fun of? How was it similar to, and how different from, this passage?

8. Think up some buffoonery with which the actors playing the watchmen can make the audience laugh.

The French Princess

The year is 1420, and the scene the palace of the King of France. King Henry V of England, convinced that the French crown is rightfully his, has brought an army into France and won a great victory at the Battle of Agincourt. While the French King is signing a treaty that will make the English King his heir, Henry himself seeks out the French Princess: if he can persuade her to marry him, there may be a stronger hope of peace between their two countries. However, since his French is poor and she knows little English, the wooing may prove difficult.

[*Enter King Henry, the Princess Katherine, and Alice, a lady attending her*]

KING HENRY   Fair Kátherine, ánd most fáir,
Will yóu vouchsáfe to téach a sóldier térms
Such ás will énter át a lády's éar,
And pléad his lóve-suit tó her géntle héart?

KATHERINE   Your Majesty shall mock at me; I cannot speak your England.

KING HENRY   O fair Katherine, if you will love me soundly with your French heart, I will be glad to hear you confess it brokenly with your English tongue. Do you like me, Kate?

KATHERINE   *Pardonnez-moi*, I cannot tell vat is like me.

KING HENRY   An angel is like you, Kate, and you are like an angel.

KATHERINE   *Que dit-il? que je suis semblable `a les anges*?

ALICE   *Oui, vraiment, sauf votre grace, ainsi dit-il.*

KING HENRY   I'faith, Kate, I am glad thou canst speak no better English; for if thou couldst, thou wouldst find me such a plain king that thou wouldst think I had sold my farm to buy my crown. I know no ways to mince it in love, but directly to say 'I love you'. Then, if you urge me farther than to say 'Do you in faith?' I wear out my suit. Give me your answer; i'faith, do; and so clap hands and a bargain. How say you, lady?

KATHERINE   *Sauf votre honneur*, me understand vell.

KING HENRY | Marry, if you would put me to verses or to dance for your sake, Kate, why you undid me. If I could win a lady at leap-frog, or by vaulting into my saddle with my armour on my back, under the correction of bragging be it spoken, I should quickly leap into a wife. But, before God, Kate, I cannot look greenly, nor gasp out my eloquence, nor I have no cunning in protestation. What! a speaker is but a prater: a rhyme is but a ballad. A good leg will fall; a straight back will stoop; a black beard will turn white; a curl'd pate will grow bald; a fair face will wither; a full eye will wax hollow. But a good heart, Kate, is the sun and moon; or, rather, the sun, and not the moon – for it shines bright and never changes, but keeps his course truly. If thou would have such a one, take me; and take me, take a soldier; take a soldier, take a king. And what say'st thou, then, to my love? Speak, my fair, and fairly, I pray thee.

KATHERINE | Is it possible dat I sould love de enemy of France?

KING HENRY | No, it is not possible you should love the enemy of France, Kate, but in loving me you should love the friend of France; for I love France so well that I will not part with a village of it; I will have it all mine. And, Kate, when France is mine and I am yours, then yours is France and you are mine.

KATHERINE | I cannot tell vat is dat.

KING HENRY | No, Kate? I will tell thee in French, which I am sure will hang upon my tongue like a new-married wife about her husband's neck, hardly to be shook off. *Quand j'ai la possession de France, et quand vous avez la possession de moi* – let me see, what then? Saint Denis be my speed! – *donc votre est France et vous ^etes mienne.* It is as easy for me, Kate, to conquer the kingdom as to speak so much more French: I shall never move thee in French, unless it be to laugh at me.

KATHERINE | *Sauf votre honneur, le Français que vous parlez, il est meilleur que l'Anglais lequel je parle.*

KING HENRY | No, faith, is't not, Kate; but thy speaking of my tongue, and I thine, most truly falsely, must needs be granted to be much at one. But, Kate, dost thou understand thus much English – Canst thou love me?

KATHERINE | I cannot tell.

KING HENRY | Can any of your neighbours tell, Kate? I'll ask them. Come, I know thou lovest me; and at night, when you come into your closet, you'll question this gentle-woman about me; and I know, Kate, you will to her dispraise those parts in me that you love with your heart. But, good Kate, mock me mercifully; the rather, gentle Princess, because I love thee cruelly. How answer you, *la plus belle Katherine du monde, mon tres ch`er et divin d´eesse?*

KATHERINE | Your *Majestee* ave *fausse* French enough to deceive de most *sage damoiselle* dat is *en France.*

KING HENRY   Now, fie upon my false French! By mine honour, in true English, I love thee, Kate; by which honour I dare not swear thou lovest me; yet my blood begins to flatter me that thou dost, notwithstanding the poor and untempering effect of my visage. Now, <u>beshrew</u> my father's   *[curse* ambition! He was thinking of civil wars when he got me; therefore was I created with a stubborn outside, with an aspect of iron, that when I come to woo ladies I fright them. But, in faith, Kate, the elder I wax, the better I shall appear: my comfort is, that old age, that ill layer-up of beauty, can do no more spoil upon my face; thou hast me, if thou hast me, at the worst; and thou shalt wear me, if thou wear me, better and better. And therefore, tell me, most fair Katherine, will you have me?

KATHERINE   Dat is as it shall please de *roi mon p`ere.*

KING HENRY   Nay, it will please him well, Kate – it shall please him, Kate.

KATHERINE   Den it sall also content me.

KING HENRY   Upon that I kiss your hand, and I call you my queen.

KATHERINE   *Laissez, mon seigneur, laissez, laissez! Les dames et demoiselles pour ˆetre bais´ees devant leur noces, il n'est pas la coutume de France.*

KING HENRY   It is not a fashion for the maids in France to kiss before they are married, would she say?

ALICE   *Oui, vraiment.*

KING HENRY   O Kate, nice customs curtsy to great kings. Dear Kate, you and I cannot be confin'd within the weak <u>list</u> of a country's fashion: we   *[bounds* are the makers of manners, Kate; therefore, patiently and yielding. [*Kissing her*]   You have witchcraft in your lips, Kate: there is more eloquence in a sugar touch of them than in the tongues of the French council; and they should sooner persuade Henry of England than a general petition of monarchs. Here comes your father.

[*Enter the French King, with English lords*]

FRENCH KING   We háve consénted tó all térms of réason.

KING HENRY   Is't só, my lórds of Éngland?

LORD   The kíng hath gránted évery árticlé:
His dáughter fírst; and thén in séquel, áll.

FRENCH KING   Táke her, fair són, and fróm her blóod raise úp
Íssue to mé; thát the conténding kíngdoms
Of Fránce and Éngland, whóse very shóres look pále
With énvy óf each óther's háppinéss,
May céase their hátred; ánd this déar conjúnction
Plant néighbourhóod and Chrístian-líke accórd
In théir sweet bósoms, that néver wár advánce
His bléeding swórd 'twixt Éngland ánd fair Fránce.

ALL   Amen!

[*Exeunt*]

[from *Henry V*, Act V, Scene ii]

Questions

1. How would you react to this wooing if you were Katherine?

2. 'I have no cunning in protestation', says King Henry. Much of his vocabulary is simple and mono-syllabic, but is there anything in the King's use of language that belies this claim?

3. 'Nice customs curtsy to great kings.' What does 'nice' mean here? How is it used nowadays?

4. How does the French King use personification in his last speech?

5. When the Princess asks 'Is it possible that I should love the enemy of France?', Henry evades the question. How would you answer her?

6. If you were playing the part of the French King would you speak his last speech as though the marriage 'pleases him well'?

7. How might the presence of the Princess's chaperone, the Lady Alice, be used to add to the comedy in this scene? How might she be characterized?

8. Have you ever had difficulty, like King Henry, in communicating with someone? Write a short dialogue between two characters who don't speak the same language.

The Recruits

Shallow and Silence, two elderly justices of the peace in Gloucestershire, have been commanded to offer more recruits to Sir John Falstaff who is marching through their county on his way to join the King's army at the battlefield. Outside Shallow's house, the five recruits they have chosen await Falstaff's verdict, their lives in the balance.

[*Enter Shallow and Silence, meeting; with Mouldy, Shadow, Wart, Feeble, Bullcalf, and Servants behind*]

SHALLOW	Come on, come on, come on, sir; give me your hand, sir; give me your hand, sir. An early stirrer, <u>by the rood</u>! And how doth [*an oath* my good cousin Silence?
SILENCE	Good morrow, good cousin Shallow.
SHALLOW	And how doth my cousin, your bedfellow? and your fairest daughter and mine, my god-daughter Ellen? I dare say my cousin William is become a good scholar; he is at Oxford still, is he not?
SILENCE	Indeed, sir, to my cost.
SHALLOW	'A must, then, to the Inns o' Court shortly. I was once of Clement's Inn; where I think they will talk of mad Shallow yet. There was I, and little John Doit of Staffordshire, and black George Barnes, and Francis Pickbone, and Will Squele a <u>Cotsole</u> man – you had not [*Cotswold* four such swinge-bucklers in all the Inns o' Court again. Then was Jack Falstaff, now Sir John, a boy, and page to Thomas Mowbray, Duke of Norfolk.
SILENCE	This Sir John, cousin, that comes hither <u>anon</u> about soldiers? [*now*
SHALLOW	The same Sir John, the very same. I see him break Scoggin's head at the court gate, when 'a was a crack not thus high; and the very same day did I fight with one Sampson Stockfish, a fruiterer, behind Gray's Inn. Jesu, Jesu, the mad days that I have spent! and to see how many of my old acquaintance are dead!
SILENCE	We shall all follow, cousin.

SHALLOW	Certain, 'tis certain; very sure, very sure. Death, as the Psalmist saith, is certain to all; all shall die. How a good yoke of bullocks at Stamford fair?
SILENCE	By my troth, I was not there.
SHALLOW	Death is certain. Is old Double of your town living yet?
SILENCE	Dead, sir.
SHALLOW	Jesu, Jesu, dead! 'A drew a good bow; and dead! 'A shot a fine shoot. John a Gaunt loved him well, and betted much money on his head. Dead! 'A would have clapp'd i' th' clout at twelve score, and carried you a forehand shaft a fourteen and a fourteen and a half, that it would have done a man's heart good to see. How a score of ewes now?
SILENCE	Thereafter as they be – a score of good ewes may be worth ten pounds.
SHALLOW	And is old Double dead?

[*Enter Falstaff and his corporal, Bardolph*]

	Look, here comes good Sir John. Give me your hand, give me your worship's good hand. Welcome, good Sir John.
FALSTAFF	I am glad to see you well, good Master Robert Shallow. Master Surecard, as I think?
SHALLOW	No, Sir John; it is my cousin Silence, in commission with me.
FALSTAFF	Good Master Silence, it well befits you should be of the peace.
SILENCE	Your good worship is welcome.
FALSTAFF	Fie! this is hot weather. Gentlemen, have you provided me here half a dozen sufficient men?
SHALLOW	Marry, have we, sir. Will you sit?
FALSTAFF	Let me see them, I beseech you.
SHALLOW	Where's the roll? Where's the roll? Where's the roll? Let me see, let me see, let me see. So, so, so, so, so – so, so – yea, marry, sir. Rafe Mouldy! Let them appear as I call; let them do so, let them do so. Let me see; where is Mouldy?
MOULDY	Here, an't please you.
SHALLOW	What think you, Sir John? A good limb'd fellow; young, strong, and of good friends.
FALSTAFF	Is thy name Mouldy?
MOULDY	Yes, an't please you.
FALSTAFF	'Tis the more time thou wert us'd.
SHALLOW	Ha, ha, ha! most excellent, i'faith! Things that are mouldy lack use. Very singular good! In faith, well said, Sir John; very well said.
FALSTAFF	Prick him.
MOULDY	I was prick'd well enough before, an you could have let me alone. My old dame will be undone now for one to <u>do her husbandry</u> [*run her house* and her drudgery. You need not to have prick'd me; there are other men fitter to go out than I.

FALSTAFF	Go to; peace, Mouldy; you shall go. Mouldy, it is time you were spent.
MOULDY	Spent!
SHALLOW	Peace, fellow, peace; stand aside; know you where you are? For th'other, Sir John – let me see. Simon Shadow!
FALSTAFF	Yea, marry, let me have him to sit under. He's like to be a cold soldier.
SHALLOW	Where's Shadow?
SHADOW	Here, sir.
SHALLOW	Do you like him, Sir John?
FALSTAFF	Shadow will serve for summer. Prick him.
SHALLOW	Thomas Wart!
FALSTAFF	Where's he?
WART	Here, sir.
FALSTAFF	Is thy name Wart?
WART	Yea, sir.
FALSTAFF	Thou art a very ragged wart.
SHALLOW	Shall I prick him, Sir John?
FALSTAFF	It were superfluous; for his apparel is built upon his back, and the whole frame stands upon pins. Prick him no more.
SHALLOW	Ha, ha, ha! You can do it sir, you can do it. I commend you well. Francis Feeble!
FEEBLE	Here, sir.
FALSTAFF	What trade art thou, Feeble?
FEEBLE	A woman's tailor, sir.
FEEBLE	Shall I prick him, sir?
FALSTAFF	You may; but if he had been a man's tailor, he'd ha' prick'd you. Wilt thou make as many holes in an enemy's battle as thou hast done in a woman's petticoat?
FEEBLE	I will do my good will, sir; you can have no more.
FALSTAFF	Well said, good woman's tailor! well said, courageous Feeble! Who is next?
SHALLOW	Peter Bullcalf o' th' green!
FALSTAFF	Yea, marry, let's see Bullcalf.
BULLCALF	Here, sir.
FALSTAFF	Fore God, a likely fellow! Come, prick me Bullcalf till he roar again.
BULLCALF	O Lord! good my lord captain –
FALSTAFF	What, dost thou roar before thou art prick'd?
BULLCALF	O Lord, sir! I am a diseased man.
FALSTAFF	What disease hast thou?
BULLCALF	A whoreson cold, sir, a cough, sir, which I caught with ringing in the King's affairs upon his coronation day, sir.
FALSTAFF	Come, thou shalt go to the wars in a gown. We will have away thy cold; and I will take such order that thy friends shall ring for thee. Is here all?

SHALLOW	Here is two more call'd than your number. You must have but four here, sir; and so, I pray you, go in with me to dinner.
FALSTAFF	Come, I will go drink with you, but I cannot <u>tarry</u> dinner.　　*[stay for* I am glad to see you, by my troth, Master Shallow.
SHALLOW	Ha, cousin Silence, that thou hadst seen that that this knight and I have seen! Ha, Sir John, said I well?
FALSTAFF	We have heard the chimes at midnight, Master Shallow.
SHALLOW	That we have, that we have, that we have; in faith, Sir John, we have. Come, let's to dinner; come, let's to dinner. Jesus, the days that we have seen! Come, come.

[Exeunt Falstaff, Shallow and Silence]

BULLCALF	Good Master Corporate Bardolph, stand my friend; and here's four Harry ten shillings in French crowns for you. In very truth, sir, I had as lief be hang'd, sir, as go. And yet, for mine own part, sir, I do not care; but rather because I am unwilling and, for mine own part, have a desire to stay with my friends; else, sir, I did not care for mine own part so much.
BARDOLPH	Go to; stand aside.
MOULDY	And, good Master Corporal Captain, for my old dame's sake, stand my friend. She has nobody to do anything about her when I am gone; and she is old, and cannot help herself. You shall have forty, sir.
BARDOLPH	Go to; stand aside.
FEEBLE	By my troth, I care not; a man can die but once; we owe God a death. I'll ne'er bear a base mind. An't be my destiny, so; an't be not, so. No man's too good to serve's Prince; and, let it go which way it will, he that dies this year is quit for the next.
BARDOLPH	Well said; th'art a good fellow.
FEEBLE	Faith, I'll bear no base mind.

[Re-enter Falstaff, Shallow and Silence]

FALSTAFF	Come, sir, which men shall I have?
SHALLOW	Four of which you please.
BARDOLPH	Sir, a word with you. I have three pound to free Mouldy and Bullcalf.
FALSTAFF	Go to; well.
SHALLOW	Come, Sir John, which four will you have?
FALSTAFF	Do you choose for me.
SHALLOW	Marry, then – Mouldy, Bullcalf, Feeble, and Shadow.
FALSTAFF	Mouldy and Bullcalf: for you, Mouldy, stay at home till you are past service; and for your part, Bullcalf, grow till you come unto it. I will none of you.
SHALLOW	Sir John, Sir John, do not yourself wrong. They are your likeliest men, and I would have you serv'd with the best.

FALSTAFF   Will you tell me, Master Shallow, how to choose a man? Care I for the limb, the thews, the stature, bulk, and big assemblance of a man! Give me the spirit, Master Shallow. [*Indicating Wart, Shadow and Feeble*] These fellows will do well. Master Shallow, God keep you! Master Silence, I will not use many words with you: Fare you well! Gentlemen both, I thank you. I must a dozen mile to-night. Bardolph, give the soldiers coats. Fare you well, gentle gentlemen. On Bardolph; lead the men away.

[*Exeunt*]

[from *Henry IV, Part Two*, Act III, Scene ii]

Questions

1. In Elizabethan English how did one greet another person, ask after someone's health, and say goodbye?

2. Suggest why Shakespeare did not put the dialogue in this scene into verse-form.

3. How might you guess that Shallow is old just from the *way* he speaks? Point out some of the characteristics of his speech.

4. Why would we not say today 'let's to dinner' or 'I must a dozen mile tonight'?

5. What exactly are Bullcalf's feelings about going to the war? Compare his response with Feeble's reasoning on the same subject.

6. What do you deduce from this scene about the character and motives of Falstaff? (Provide detailed evidence from the text in support of your views.)

7. Why do you think Shakespeare may have chosen for the opening of this scene a conversation about death between two old men?

8. If you were staging this scene, how would you want the five recruits to look, sound and move?

9. What is there here to make you laugh? Is there anything to make you sad or angry?

Winter

When íciclés hang bý the wáll,
And Díck the shépherd blóws his náil,
And Tóm bears lógs intó the háll,
And mílk comes frózen hóme in páil,
When blóod is nípp'd, and wáys be fóul,
Then níghtly síngs the stáring ówl:
'Tu-whó;
Tu-whít, tu-whó' – A mérry nóte,
While gréasy Jóan doth kéel the pót.

When áll alóud the wínd doth blów,
And cóughing dRówns the párson's <u>sáw</u>,   [*wisdom*
And bírds sit bróoding ín the snów,
And Márian's nóse looks réd and ráw,
When róasted <u>crábs</u> hiss ín the bówl,   [*crab apples*
Then níghtly síngs the stáring ówl:
'Tu-whó;
Tu-whít, Tu-whó' – A mérry nóte,
While gréasy Jóan doth kéel the pót.

[from *Love's Labour's Lost*, Act V, Scene ii]

Practice

This poem is composed of two nine-line verses.

Each line – except of course 'Tu-who' – seems to have four heavier stresses in an iambic rhythm (i.e., $-/-/-/-/$).

The first line of each verse rhymes with the third; the second line rhymes with the fourth; and the fifth line rhymes with the sixth.

The last three lines of each verse are identical, and so may be called a 'refrain'.

Write a poem of your own describing one of the four seasons as vividly as Shakespeare has. Try to use the same metrical pattern.

Richard and Bolingbroke

In 1399, King Richard II returns from wars in Ireland to find that his banished cousin, Henry Bolingbroke, has invaded England and won over the nobles to his cause. Although Bolingbroke protests that he has come only to claim the dukedom that is his since his father's death, Richard has no doubt of his *real* intentions. The King and his few remaining friends have taken refuge in Flint Castle.

[*Enter at one side Bolingbroke, the Earl of Northumberland, and Soldiers. Northumberland advances to the castle walls, and trumpets sound a parle.*

Flourish. Enter on the walls above, King Richard, the Duke of Aumerle, and Lords.]

KING RICHARD [*To Northumberland, below*]

We áre amáz'd; and thús long háve we stóod
To wátch the féarful bénding óf thy knée,
Becáuse we thóught oursélf thy láwful kíng;
And íf we bé, how dáre thy jóints forgét
To páy their áwful dúty tó our présence?
If wé be nót, show ús the hánd of Gód
That háth dismíss'd us fróm our stéwardshíp;
For wéll we knów no hánd of blóod and bóne
Can grípe the sácred hándle óf our scéptre,
Unléss he dó profáne, stéal, or usúrp.
And thóugh you thínk that áll, as yóu have dóne,
Have tórn their sóuls by túrning thém from ús,
And wé are bárren ánd beréft of fríends,
Yet knów – my máster, Gód omnípotént,
Is mústering ín his clóuds on óur behálf
Ármies of péstilénce; and théy shall stríke
Your chíldren yét unbórn and únbegót,
That líft your <u>vással</u> hánds agáinst my héad   [*subject, servant*
And thréat the glóry óf my précious crówn.
Tell Bólingbróke, for yón methínks he stánds,
That évery stríde he mákes upón my lánd
Is dángerous tréason.

NORTHUMBERLAND   Thý thrice nóble cóusin,
Hárry Bolingbróke, doth húmbly kíss thy hánd;
And bý the hónouráble tómb he swéars
That stánds upón your róyal grándsire's bónes,
And bý the róyaltíes of bóth your blóods,
His cóming híther háth no fúrther scópe
Than fór his líneal róyalties, ánd to bég
Enfránchisemént immédiate ón his knées;
Whích on thy róyal párty gránted ónce,
His glíttering árms he wíll comménd to rúst,
His bárbëd stéeds to stábles, ánd his héart   [*armour-covered*
To fáithful sérvice óf your Májestý.
This swéars he, ás he ís a prínce, is júst;
And ás I ám a géntlemán I crédit hím.

KING RICHARD   Northúmberlánd, say thús the Kíng retúrns:
His nóble cóusin ís right wélcome híther;
And áll the númber óf his fáir demánds
Shall bé accómplish'd wíthout cóntradíction.
With áll the grácious útteránce thou hást
Spéak to his géntle héaring kínd comménds.
[*To Aumerle*]   We dó debáse oursélves, cóusin, dó we nót,
To lóok so póorly ánd to spéak so fáir?
Sháll we call báck Northúmberlánd, and sénd
Defíance tó the tráitor, ánd so díe?

AUMERLE   Nó, good my lórd; let's fíght with géntle wórds
Till tíme lend fríends, and fríends their hélpful swórds.

KING RICHARD   O Gód, O Gód! that é'er this tóngue of míne
That láid the séntence óf dread bánishmént
On yón proud mán should táke it óff agáin
With wórds of sóoth! O thát I wére as gréat   [*flattery*
As ís my gríef, or lésser thán my náme!
Or thát I cóuld forgét what Í have béen!
Or nót remémber whát I múst be nów!

AUMERLE   Northúmberlánd comes báck from Bólingbróke.

KING RICHARD | Whát must the Kíng do nów? Múst he submít?
The Kíng shall dó it. Múst he bé depós'd?
The Kíng shall bé conténted. Múst he lóse
The náme of kíng? <u>A Gód's name</u>, lét it gó.   [*freely, gladly*
I'll gíve my jéwels fór a sét of béads,
My górgeous pálace fór a hérmitáge,
My gáy appárel fór an <u>álmsman's</u> gówn,   [*hermit's*
My fígur'd góblets fór a dísh of wóod,
My scéptre fór a pálmer's wálking stáff
My súbjects fór a páir of cárvëd sáints,
And mý large kíngdom fór a líttle gráve,
A líttle líttle gráve, an óbscure gráve –
Or Í'll be búried ín the kíng's highwáy,
Some wáy of cómmon tráde, where súbjects' féet
May hóurly trámple ón their sóvereign's héad;
For ón my héart they tréad now whílst I líve,
And búried ónce, why nót upón my héad?
Most míghty prínce, my Lórd Northúmberlánd,
What sáys King Bólingbroke? Wíll his Májestý
Give Ríchard léave to líve till Ríchard díe?
You máke a lég, and Bólingbróke says áy.

NORTHUMBERLAND | My lórd, ín the base cóurt he dóth atténd
To spéak with yóu; may it pléase you tó come dówn?

KING RICHARD | Down, dówn I cóme, like glíst'ring <u>Pháethón</u>,   [*Phaethon, in Greek mythology, could not control the chariot of the sun*
Wánting the mánage óf unrúly <u>jádes</u>.   [*horses*
Ín the base cóurt? Base cóurt, where kíngs grow báse,
To cóme at tráitors' cálls, and dó them gráce.
Ín the base cóurt? Come dówn? Down, coúrt! down, kíng!
For níght-owls shríek where móunting lárks should síng.

[*Exeunt those above*]

BOLINGBROKE | What sáys his Májestý?

NORTHUMBERLAND | Sórrow and gríef of héart
Máke him speak fóndly, líke a frántic mán;
Yét he is cóme.

[*Enter the King, and his attendants, below*]

BOLINGBROKE | Stand áll apárt,
And shów fair dúty tó his Májestý.   [*Kneels*]
My grácious lórd –

KING RICHARD   Fair cóusin, yoú debáse your príncely knée
                            To máke the báse earth próud with kíssing ít.*
                            Up, cóusin, úp; your héart is úp, I knów,
                            [*Touching his own head*]
                            Thus hígh at léast, althóugh your knée be lów.
                            Set ón towards Lóndon. Cóusin, ís it só?
BOLINGBROKE   Yéa, my good lórd.
KING RICHARD   Then Í must nót say nó.

                                      [*Flourish. Exeunt*]

                              [from *Richard II*, Act III, Scene iii]

NOTE

*The French word for 'kiss' is *baiser*.

Questions

1. What does Shakespeare gain by setting this scene on the castle walls?

2. What is it in the language of Richard's first speech that makes him sound so regal there?

3. Show how Shakespeare re-arranges normal word-order in Northumberland's first speech.

4. Aumerle wants Richard to use 'gentle words'. Does he?

5. 'And my large kingdom for a little grave.' Is this line what we expect for the climax to the speech?

6. To Northumberland, Richard sounds 'like a frantic man'. How far would you agree?

7. Why does Shakespeare give Bolingbroke so little to say?

Taming the Shrew

Katherina is known all over Padua for the violence of her temper and, even though her father will give half his fortune to her husband, no one can be found willing to marry her; not until a cheerful stranger called Petruchio arrives in the town. Delighted with the prospect of the dowry and paying no heed to any warning, he marries the 'shrew' without delay; then, ignoring her furious protests, he drags her off to his house in the country, there to begin her reformation.

[Enter Grumio, a servant]

GRUMIO   Fie, fie on all tired <u>jades</u>, on all mad masters, and all foul   [*horses* ways! Was ever man so beaten? Was ever man so weary? I am sent before to make a fire, and they are coming after to warm them. Now were not I a little pot and soon hot, my very lips might freeze to my teeth, my tongue to the roof of my mouth, my heart in my belly, ere I should come by a fire to thaw me. But I with blowing the fire shall warm myself; for, considering the weather, a taller man than I will take cold. Holla, ho! Curtis!

[Enter Curtis]

CURTIS   Who is that calls so coldly?

GRUMIO   A piece of ice. If thou doubt it, thou mayst slide from my shoulder to my heel with no greater a run but my head and my neck. A fire, good Curtis.

CURTIS   Is my master and his wife coming, Grumio?

GRUMIO   O, ay, Curtis, ay; and therefore fire, fire; cast on no water.

CURTIS   Is she so hot a shrew as she's reported?

GRUMIO   She was, good Curtis, before this frost; but thou know'st winter tames man, woman, and beast; for it hath tam'd my old master, and my new mistress, and myself, fellow Curtis. But wilt thou make a fire, or shall I complain on thee to our mistress, whose hand – she being now at hand – thou shalt soon feel, to thy cold comfort, for being slow in thy hot office?

CURTIS   I prithee, good Grumio, tell me how goes the world?

GRUMIO	A cold world, Curtis, in every office but thine; and therefore fire. Do thy duty, and have thy duty, for my master and mistress are almost frozen to death.
CURTIS	There's fire ready; and therefore, good Grumio, the news?
GRUMIO	Where's the cook? Is supper ready, the house trimm'd, rushes strew'd, cobwebs swept, the serving-men in their new <u>fustian</u>, [*a type of cloth* their white stockings, and every officer his wedding-garment on?
CURTIS	All ready; and therefore, I pray thee, news.
GRUMIO	First know my horse is tired; my master and mistress fall'n out.
CURTIS	How?
GRUMIO	Out of their saddles into the dirt; and thereby hangs a tale.
CURTIS	Let's ha't, good Grumio.
GRUMIO	Lend thine ear.
CURTIS	Here.
GRUMIO	There. [*Striking him*]
CURTIS	This 'tis to feel a tale, not to hear a tale.
GRUMIO	And therefore 'tis call'd a sensible tale; and this cuff was but to knock at your ear and beseech list'ning. Now I begin: <u>Imprimis</u>, we [*first* came down a foul hill, my master riding behind my mistress –
CURTIS	Both of one horse?
GRUMIO	What's that to thee?
CURTIS	Why, a horse.
GRUMIO	Tell thou the tale. But hadst thou not cross'd me, thou shouldst have heard how her horse fell and she under her horse; thou shouldst have heard in how miry a place, how she was bemoil'd, how he left her with the horse upon her, how he beat me because her horse stumbled, how she waded through the dirt to pluck him off me, how he swore, how she pray'd that never pray'd before, how I cried, how the horses ran away, how her bridle was burst, how I lost my crupper – with many things of worthy memory, which now shall die in oblivion, and thou return unexperienc'd to thy grave.
CURTIS	By this reck'ning he is more shrew than she.
GRUMIO	Ay, and that thou and the proudest of you all shall find when he comes home. But what talk I of this? Call forth Nathaniel, Joseph, Nicholas, Philip, Walter, Sugarsop, and the rest; let their heads be sleekly comb'd, their blue coats brush'd and their garters of an indifferent knit. Are they all ready?
CURTIS	They are.
GRUMIO	Call them forth.
CURTIS	Do you hear, ho?

[*Enter four or five Servants*]

NATHANIEL	Welcome home, Grumio!
PHILIP	How now, Grumio!
JOSEPH	What, Grumio!
NICHOLAS	Fellow Grumio!
NATHANIEL	How now, old lad!
GRUMIO	Welcome, you! – how now, you! – what, you! – fellow, you! – and thus much for greeting. Now, my spruce companions, is all ready, and all things neat?
NATHANIEL	All things is ready. How near is our master?
GRUMIO	E'en at hand, alighted by this; and therefore be not –
	<u>Cock's passion</u>, silence! I hear my master. [*an oath*

[*Enter Petruchio and Katherina*]

PETRUCHIO	Where bé these knáves? Whát, no mán at dóor	
	To hóld my stírrup nór to táke my hórse!	
	Whére is Nathániel, Grégory, Phílip?	
ALL	Here, here, sir; here, sir.	
PETRUCHIO	Here, sir! here, sir! here, sir! here, sir!	
	You lógger-héaded ánd unpólish'd gróoms!	
	What, nó atténdance? nó regárd? no dúty?	
	Whére is the fóolish <u>knáve</u> I sént befóre?	[*villain*
GRUMIO	Hére, sir; as fóolish ás I wás befóre.	
PETRUCHIO	You péasant <u>swáin</u>! you whóreson mált-horse drúdge!	[*fool*
	Did Í not bíd thee méet me ín the párk	
	And bríng alóng these ráscal knáves with thée?	
GRUMIO	Nathániel's cóat, sir, wás not fúlly máde,	
	And Gábriel's púmps were áll <u>unpínk'd</u> i' th' héel;	[*frayed*
	There wás no <u>línk</u> to cólour Péter's hát,	[*a torch – the hat*
	And Wálter's dágger wás not cóme from shéathing;	*would be blackened*
	There wás none fíne but Ádam, Rálph, and Grégory;	*with the smoke*
	The rést were rágged, óld, and béggarlý;	*from it*
	Yet, ás they áre, here áre they cóme to méet you.	
PETRUCHIO	Go, ráscals, gó and fétch my súpper ín.	

[*Exeunt some of the Servants*]

[*Sings*]   Where is the life that late I led?
                    Where are those –

Sit down, Kate, and welcome.

[*Re-enter Servants with supper*]

PETRUCHIO
(continued)

Why, whén, I sáy? Nay, góod sweet Káte, be mérry.
Óff with my bóots, you rógues! you víllains, whén?

[*Sings*]　It was the friar of orders grey,
　　　　As he forth walked on his way –

Óut, you rógue, you plúck my fóot awrý;
Take thát, and ménd the plúcking óff the óther.

[*Strikes him*]

Be mérry, Káte. Some wáter, hére, what, hó!

[*Enter a Servant with water*]

Whére's my spániel Tróilus? Sírrah, gét you hénce,
And bíd my cóusin Férdinánd come híther:

[*Exit Servant*]

One, Káte, that yóu must kíss and bé acquáinted with.
Whére are my slíppers? Sháll I háve some wáter?
Come, Káte, and wásh, and wélcome héartilý.
You whóreson víllain! wíll you lét it fáll?

[*Strikes him*]

KATHERINA

Pátience, I práy you; 'twás a fáult unwílling.

PETRUCHIO

A whóreson, béetle-héaded, fláp-ear'd knáve!
Come, Káte, sit dówn; I knów you háve a <u>stómach</u>.

[*appetite*

Will yóu give thánks, sweet Káte, or élse shall Í?
What's thís? Mútton?

1ST SERVANT

　　　　　　　　Áy.

PETRUCHIO

　　　　　　　　　　Who bróught it?

PETER

　　　　　　　　　　　　　Í

PETRUCHIO

'Tis búrnt; and só is áll the méat.
What dógs are thése? Whére is the ráscal cóok?
How dúrst you víllains bríng it fróm the drésser
And sérve it thús to mé that lóve it nót?
There, táke it tó you, <u>trénchers</u>, cúps, and áll;

[*plates*

[*Throws the meat, etc., at them*]

You héedless jóltheads ánd unmánner'd sláves!
Whát, do you grúmble? Í'll be wíth you stráight.

[*Exeunt Servants*]

KATHERINA   I práy you, húsband, bé not só disquíet;
                        The méat was wéll, if yóu were só conténted.

PETRUCHIO   I téll thee, Káte, 'twas búrnt and dríed awáy.
                        Be pátient; to-mórrow't sháll be ménded,
                        And fór this níght we'll fást for cómpaný.
                        Come, Í will bríng thee tó thy brídal chámber.

[Exeunt. Re-enter Servants]

NATHANIEL   Peter, didst ever see the like?

PETER   He kills her in her own humour.

CURTIS   He ráils, and swéars, and rátes, that shé, poor sóul,
                        Knows nót which wáy to stánd, to lóok, to spéak,
                        And síts as óne new rísen fróm a dréam.
                        Awáy, awáy, for hé is cóming híther.

[Exeunt. Re-enter Petruchio]

PETRUCHIO   Thus háve I póliticlý begún my réign,
                        And 'tís my hópe to énd succéssfullý.
                        She éat no méat to-dáy, nor nóne shall éat;
                        Last níght she slépt not, nór to-níght she sháll not;
                        Ás with the méat, some úndesérvëd fáult
                        I'll fínd abóut the máking óf the béd;
                        And hére I'll flíng the píllow, thére the bólster,
                        This wáy the cóverlet, anóther wáy the shéets;
                        Áy and amíd this húrly Í inténd
                        That áll is dóne in réverend cáre of hér –
                        And, ín conclúsion, shé shall wátch all níght;
                        And íf she chánce to nód I'll ráil and bráwl
                        And wíth the clámour kéep her stíll awáke.
                        Thís is a wáy to kíll a wífe with kíndness,
                        And thús I'll cúrb her mád and héadstrong húmour.
                        Hé that knows bétter hów to táme a shréw,
                        Now lét him spéak; 'tis cháritý to shów.

[Exit]

[from *Taming of the Shrew*, Act IV, Scene i]

Questions

1. Explain how Grumio makes us laugh. How does he use exaggeration, illogicality, word-play, and other techniques?

2. Why does Grumio say that Curtis will 'return' to his grave?

3. Why does Shakespeare make us wait so long to see Petruchio and Katherina? How do you imagine Katherina is looking and feeling at her entrance?

4. When does Shakespeare begin to use verse in this scene, and why?

5. What do the words 'sensible' and 'humour' mean here? What would we use today instead?

6. What terms does Petruchio use to, and about, his servants? How does he address Katherina? Is there any evidence of how he *normally* treats his servants?

7. If you were directing a performance of this scene, what would you have Katherina do while her husband berates the servants?

8. Find an example of a paradox in Petruchio's last speech.

9. Who or what is Cousin Ferdinand supposed to be?

10. Do you think Katherina will see through her husband's pretence of 'reverend care' for her? Imagine what she might have to say to her father when she next meets him, and write a speech for her at that meeting, using the style of the verse in this scene if you can.

Part Two

The Brothers

[from *The Comedy of Errors*]

The action takes place in Ephesus, a city near the Aegean coast of what is now Turkey – an ancient and mysterious city then known for sorcery and the black arts.

Antipholus of Syracuse is travelling the world in search of his long-lost twin brother, who was separated from him in a shipwreck many years ago. In the same shipwreck his servant, Dromio, also lost a twin brother. The two of them have just arrived in Ephesus, and Antipholus is talking to a local merchant who has some money of his . . .

Scene 1

[*Scene: a street in the city. Enter Antipholus of Syracuse, Dromio of Syracuse, and a Merchant*]

MERCHANT   Thére is your móney thát I hád to kéep.

ANTIPHOLUS OF S. Go béar it tó the Céntaur, whére we hóst.
And stáy there, Drómio, tíll I cóme to thée.
Withín this hóur it wíll be dínner-tíme;
Till thát, I'll víew the mánners óf the tówn,
Perúse the tráders, gáze upón the búildings,
And thén retúrn and sléep withín mine ínn;
For wíth long trável Í am stíff and wéary.
Get thée awáy.

[*Exit Dromio of S.*]

A trústy víllain, sír, that véry óft,
When Í am dúll with cáre and mélanchóly,
Líghtens my húmour wíth his mérry jésts.
What, wíll you wálk with mé abóut the tówn,
And thén go tó my ínn and díne with mé?

MERCHANT   I ám invíted, sír, to cértain mérchants,
                  Of whóm I hópe to máke much bénefít;
                  I cráve your párdon. Sóon at fíve o'clóck,
                  Pléase you, I'll méet with yóu upón the <u>márt</u>,   [*market*
                  And áfterwárd consórt you tíll bed-tíme.
                  My présent búsiness cálls me fróm you nów.
ANTIPHOLUS OF S. Farewéll till thén. I wíll go lóse mysélf,
                  And wánder úp and dówn to víew the cíty.
MERCHANT   Sir, Í commént you tó your ówn contént.

                                                          [*Exit Merchant*]

ANTIPHOLUS OF S. Hé that comménds me tó mine ówn contént
                  Comménds me tó the thíng I cánnot gét.
                  Í to the wórld am líke a dróp of wáter
                  That ín the ócean séeks anóther dróp,
                  Who, fáiling thére to fínd his féllow fórth,
                  Unséen, inquísitíve, confóunds himsélf.
                  So Í, to fínd my bróther, lóst at séa,
                  And mý man Drómio's bróther, wréck'd with hím,
                  In qúest of thém, unháppy, lóse mysélf.
                  Five súmmers háve I spént in fárthest Gréece,
                  Róaming clean thróugh the bóunds of Ásiá,
                  And, cóasting hómeward, cóme to Éphesús;
                  Hópeless to fínd, yet lóath to léave unsóught
                  Or thát or ány pláce that hárbours mén.

                  [*Enter Dromio of Ephesus*]

                  What nów? How chánce thou árt retúrn'd so sóon?
DROMIO OF E.   Retúrn'd so sóon! ráther appróach'd too láte.
                  The cápon búrns, the píg falls fróm the spít;
                  The clóck hath strúcken twélve upón the béll –
                  My místress máde it óne upón my chéek;
                  She ís so hót becáuse the méat is cóld,
                  The méat is cóld becáuse you cóme not hóme –
ANTIPHOLUS OF S. Whére have you léft the móney thát I gáve you?
DROMIO OF E.   O – síxpence thát I hád a Wédnesday lást
                  To páy the sáddler fór my místress' crúpper?
                  The sáddler hád it, sír; I képt it nót.
ANTIPHOLUS OF S. I ám not ín a spórtive húmour nów;
                  Téll me, and dálly nót, whére is the móney?
                  Wé being strángers hére, how dár'st thou trúst
                  So gréat a chárge from thíne own cústodý?

DROMIO OF E. I práy you jést, sir, ás you sít at dínner.
Í from my místress cóme to yóu in póst;
If Í retúrn, I sháll be póst indeéd,
For shé will scóre your fáult upón my páte. [*head*

ANTIPHOLUS OF S. Come, Drómio, cóme, these jésts are óut of séason;
Resérve them tíll a mérrier hóur than thís.
Whére is the góld I gáve in chárge to thée?

DROMIO OF E. To mé, sir? Whý, you gáve no góld to mé.

ANTIPHOLUS OF S. Come ón, sir knáve, have dóne your fóolishnéss,
And téll me hów thou hást dispós'd thy chárge.

DROMIO OF E. My chárge was bút to fétch you fróm the márt
Hóme to your hóuse, the Phóenix, sír, to dínner.
My místress ánd her síster stáys for yóu.

ANTIPHOLUS OF S. Nów, as I ám a Chrístian, ánswer mé
In whát safe pláce you háve bestów'd my móney,
Or Í shall bréak that mérry scónce of yóurs, [*head*
That stánds on trícks when Í am úndispós'd.
Whére is the thóusand márks thou hádst of mé? [*coins*

DROMIO OF E. I háve some márks of yóurs upón my páte,
Sóme of my místress' márks upón my shóulders,
But nót a thóusand márks betwéen you bóth.

ANTIPHOLUS OF S. Thy místress' márks! What místress, sláve, hast thóu?

DROMIO OF E. Your wórship's wífe, my místress át the Phóenix;
Shé that doth fást till yóu come hóme to dínner,
And práys that yóu will híe you hóme to dínner.

ANTIPHOLUS OF S. Whát, wilt thou flóut me thús untó my fáce,
Béing forbíd? There, táke you thát, sir knáve.

[*Beats him*]

DROMIO OF E. What méan you, sír? For Gód's sake hóld your hánds!
Náy, an you wíll not, sír, I'll táke my héels.

[*Exit Dromio of E.*]

ANTIPHOLUS OF S. Upón my lífe, by sóme devíce or óther
The víllain ís o'er-ráught of áll my móney.
They sáy this tówn is fúll of cózenáge; [*trickery*
As, nímble júgglers thát decéive the éye,
Dark-wórking sórcerérs that chánge the mínd,
Soul-kílling wítches thát defórm the bódy,
Disgúisëd chéaters, práting móuntebánks, [*rogues*
And mány súch-like líbertíes of sín;
If ít prove só, I wíll be góne the sóoner.
I'll tó the Céntaur tó go séek this sláve.
I gréatly féar my móney ís not sáfe.

[*Exit*]

Scene 2

[Scene: the house of Antipholus of Ephesus. Enter Adriana and Luciana, her sister]

ADRIANA Néither my húsband nór the sláve retúrn'd
      That ín such háste I sént to séek his máster!
      Sure, Lúciána, ít is twó o'clóck.

LUCIANA Here cómes your mán, nów is your húsband nígh.

[Enter Dromio of Ephesus]

ADRIANA Sáy, is your <u>tárdy</u> máster nów at hánd?   *[late*

DROMIO OF E. Nay, he's at two hands with me, and that my two ears can witness.

ADRIANA But sáy, I príthee, ís he cóming hóme?
      It séems he háth great cáre to pléase his wífe.

DROMIO OF E. When Í desír'd him tó come hóme to dínner,
      He ásk'd me fór a thóusand márks in góld.
      ''Tis dínner tíme' quoth Í; 'My góld!' quoth hé.
      'Your méat doth búrn' quoth Í; 'My góld!' quoth hé.
      'Will yóu come hóme?' quoth Í; 'My góld!' quoth hé.
      'Whére is the thóusand márks I gáve thee, víllain?'
      'The píg' quoth Í 'is búrn'd.' 'My góld!' quoth hé.
      'My místress, sír' quoth Í; 'Hang úp thy místress;
      'I know nót thy místress; óut on thy místress.'

LUCIANA Quoth who?

DROMIO OF E. Quoth my master.
      'I knów' quoth hé 'no hóuse, no wífe, no místress.'

ADRIANA Go báck agáin, thou sláve, and fétch him hóme.

DROMIO OF E. Go báck agáin, and bé new béaten hóme?
      For Gód's sake, sénd some óther méssengér.

ADRIANA Back, sláve, or Í will bréak thy páte across.

DROMIO OF E. And hé will bléss that cróss with óther béating;
      Betwéen you Í shall háve a hóly héad.

ADRIANA Hence práting péasant! Fétch thy máster hóme.

[Exeunt]

Scene 3

[*Scene: a street in the city. Enter Antipholus of Syracuse*]

ANTIPHOLUS OF S. The góld I gáve to Drómio ís laid úp
Sáfe at the Céntaur, ánd the héedful sláve
Is wánd'red fórth in cáre to séek me óut.

[*Enter Dromio of Syracuse*]

How nów, sir, ís your mérry húmour álter'd?
As yóu love strókes, so jést with mé agáin.
You knów no Céntaur! Yóu recéiv'd no góld!
Your místress sént to háve me hóme to dínner!
My hóuse was át the Phóenix! Wást thou mád,
That thús so mádly thóu didst ánswer mé?

DROMIO OF S. What ánswer, sír? When spáke I súch a wórd?

ANTIPHOLUS OF S. Even nów, even hére, not hálf an hóur sínce.

DROMIO OF S. I díd not sée you sínce you sént me hénce,
Hóme to the Céntaur, wíth the góld you gáve me.

ANTIPHOLUS OF S. Víllain, thou dídst denÿ the góld's recéipt,
And tóld'st me óf a místress ánd a dínner;
For whích, I hópe, thou félt'st I wás displéas'd.

DROMIO OF S. I am glád to sée you ín this mérry véin.
What méans this jést? I práy you, máster, téll me.

ANTIPHOLUS OF S. Yea, dóst thou jéer and flóut me ín the téeth?
Think'st thóu I jést? Hold, táke thou thát, and thát.

[*Beating him*]

DROMIO OF S. Hóld, sir, for Gód's sake! Nów your jést is éarnest.

ANTIPHOLUS OF S. Becáuse that Í famíliarlÿ sometímes
Do úse you fór my fóol and chát with yóu,
Your sáucinéss will jést upón my lóve,
And máke a cómmon óf my sérious hóurs.
Whén the sun shínes let fóolish gnáts make spórt,
But créep in cránnies whén he hídes his béams.
But, sóft, who wáfts us yónder?

[*Enter Adriana and Luciana*]

ADRIANA   Ay, áy, Antípholús, look stránge and fdrówn.
                 Í am not Ádriána, nór thy wífe.
                 The tíme was ónce when thóu unúrg'd wouldst vów
                 That néver wórds were músic tó thine éar,
                 That néver óbject pléasing ín thine éye,
                 That néver tóuch well wélcome tó thy hánd,
                 That néver méat sweet-sávour'd ín thy táste,
                 Unléss I spáke, or lóok'd, or tóuch'd, or cárv'd to thée.
                 How cómes it nów, my húsband, Ó, how cómes it,
                 That thóu art thén estrángëd fróm thysélf?

ANTIPHOLUS OF S. Pléad you to mé, fair dáme? I knów you nót:
                 In Éphesús I ám but twó hours óld,
                 As stránge untó your tówn as tó your tálk.

LUCIANA   Fie, bróther, hów the wórld is cháng'd with yóu!
                 When wére you wónt to úse my síster thús?
                 She sént for yóu by Drómio hóme to dínner.

ANTIPHOLUS OF S. By Dromio?

DROMIO OF S.   By me?

ADRIANA   By thée; and thís thou dídst retúrn from hím –
                 That hé did búffet thée, and ín his blóws
                 Deníed my hóuse for hís, mé for his wífe.

ANTIPHOLUS OF S. Did yóu convérse, sir, wíth this géntlewóman?

DROMIO OF S.   Í, sir? I néver sáw her tíll this tíme.

ANTIPHOLUS OF S. Víllain, thou líest; for éven her véry wórds
                 Didst thóu delíver tó me ón the márt.

DROMIO OF S.   I néver spáke with hér in áll my lífe.

ANTIPHOLUS OF S. How cán she thús, then, cáll us bý our námes?

LUCIANA   Drómio, go bíd the sérvants spréad for dínner.

ADRIANA   Come, sír, to dínner. Drómio, kéep the gáte.
                 Húsband, I'll díne abóve with yóu to-dáy.
                 Sírrah, if ány ásk you fór your máster,
                 Sáy he dines fórth, and lét no créature énter.
                 Come, síster. Drómio pláy the pórter wéll.

ANTIPHOLUS OF S. [*Aside*]   Am Í in éarth, in héaven, ór in héll?
                 Sléeping or wáking, mád or wéll-advís'd?
                 Knówn unto thése, and tó mysélf disguís'd!
                 I'll sáy as théy say, ánd perséver só,
                 And ín this míst at áll advéntures gó.

DROMIO OF S.   Máster, shall Í be pórter át the gáte?

ADRIANA   Áy; and lét none énter, lést I bréak your páte.

LUCIANA   Come, cóme, Antípholús, we díne too láte.

                                                        [*Exeunt*]

Scene 4

[Scene: *before the house of Antipholus of Ephesus. Enter Antipholus of Ephesus, Dromio of Ephesus, Angelo and Balthazar, two merchants. Dromio of Syracuse within*]

ANTIPHOLUS OF E. Good Sígnior Ángelo, you múst excúse us áll;
My wífe is shréwish whén I kéep not hóurs.
But hére's a víllain thát would fáce me dówn
He mét me ón the márt, and thát I béat him,
And chárg'd him wíth a thóusand márks in góld,
And thát I díd dený my wífe and hóuse.
Thou drúnkard, thóu, what dídst thou méan by thís?

DROMIO OF E. Say whát you wíll, sir, but Í know whát I knów.
· That you béat me at the márt I háve your hánd to shów.
If the skín were párchment, and the blóws you gáve were ínk,
Your ówn handwríting would téll you whát I thínk.

ANTIPHOLUS OF E. I thínk thou árt an áss.

DROMIO OF E.   Marry, só it dóth appéar
By the wróngs I súffer ánd the blóws I béar.

ANTIPHOLUS OF E. But, sóft, my dóor is lóck'd; go bíd them lét us ín.

DROMIO OF E. What pátch is máde our pórter? My máster stáys in the stréet.

DROMIO OF S. [*Within*]   Let him wálk from whénce he cáme, lest hé catch cóld
                                                          on's féet.

ANTIPHOLUS OF E. Who tálks withín there? Ho, ópen the dóor.

DROMIO OF S. [*Within*]   Ríght, sir; I'll téll you whén, an yóu'll tell mé wherefóre.

ANTIPHOLUS OF E. Whérefore? For my dínner; I háve not dín'd to-dáy.

DROMIO OF S. [*Within*]   Nor to-dáy here you múst not; come agáin when you máy.

ANTIPHOLUS OF E. What art thóu that kéep'st me óut from the hóuse I ówe.

DROMIO OF S. [*Within*]   The pórter for this tíme, sir, and my náme is Drómió.

DROMIO OF E. O víllain, thou hast stól'n both mine óffice and my náme!

[*Enter Adriana, within*]

ADRIANA [*Within*]   Who ís that át the dóor, thát keeps áll this nóise?

DROMIO OF S. [*Within*]   By my tróth, your tówn is tróubled wíth unrúly bóys.

ANTIPHOLUS OF E. Are yóu there, wífe? You míght have cóme befóre.

ADRIANA [*Within*]   Your wífe, sir knáve! Go gét you fróm the dóor.

ANTIPHOLUS OF E. Go fétch me sómething; Í'll break ópe the gáte.

DROMIO OF S. [*Within*]   Break ány bréaking hére, and Í'll break yóur knave's páte.

ANTIPHOLUS OF E. Go gét thee góne; fetch mé an íron crów.

BALTHAZAR Have pátience, sír; O lét it nót be só!
Be rúl'd by mé: depárt in patiénce,
And lét us tó the Tíger áll to dínner;
Ánd, about évening, cóme yoursélf alóne
To knów the réason óf this stránge restráint.

ANTIPHOLUS OF E. You háve preváil'd. I wíll depárt in quíet,
Since míne own dóors refúse to éntertáin me,
I'll knóck elsewhére, to sée if théy'll disdáin me.

[*Exeunt*]

Scene 5

The twin brothers are constantly mistaken for one another by the citizens of Ephesus, who cannot understand their strange behaviour and decide that Antipholus must be mad. Adriana calls in one Doctor Pinch.

[*Scene: a street in the city. Enter Adriana, Luciana, Pinch and citizens, meeting Antipholus of Ephesus and Dromio of Ephesus.*]

ADRIANA	Good Dóctor Pínch, you áre a <u>cónjurér</u>: [*exorcist*
	Estáblish hím in hís true sénse agáin,
	And Í will pléase you whát you wíll demánd.
LUCIANA	Alás, how fíery ánd how shárp he lóoks!
PINCH	Gíve me your hánd, and lét it féel your púlse.
ANTIPHOLUS OF E.	Thére is my hánd, and lét it féel your éar.

[*Striking him*]

PINCH	I chárge thee, Sátan, hóus'd withín this mán,
	To yíeld posséssion tó my hóly práyers,
	And tó thy státe of dárkness híe thee stráight.
	I cónjure thée by áll the sáints in héaven.
ANTIPHOLUS OF E.	Péace, doting wízard, péace! I ám not mád.
ADRIANA	O thát thou wért not, póor distréssëd sóul!
ANTIPHOLUS OF E.	You <u>mínion</u>, yóu, are thése your cústomérs? [*harlot*
	Did thís compánion wíth the sáffron fáce
	Rével and féast it át my hóuse to-dáy,
	Whílst upon mé the guílty dóors were shút,
	And Í deníed to énter ín my hóuse?
ADRIANA	O húsband, Gód doth knów you dín'd at hóme,
	Where wóuld you hád remáin'd untíl this tíme,
	Frée from these slánders ánd this ópen sháme!
ANTIPHOLUS OF E.	Dín'd at hóme! Thou, víllain, whát sayest thóu?
DROMIO OF E.	Sir, sóoth to sáy, you díd not díne at hóme.
ANTIPHOLUS OF E.	Were nót my dóors lock'd úp and Í shut óut?
DROMIO OF E.	<u>Perdíe</u>, your dóors were lóck'd and yóu shut óut. [*an oath*
ANTIPHOLUS OF E.	And díd not Í in ráge depárt from thénce?
DROMIO OF E.	In vérití, you díd. My bónes bear wítness,
	That sínce have félt the vígour óf his ráge.
PINCH	Místress, both mán and máster ís posséss'd;
	I knów it bý their pále and déadly lóoks.
	They múst be bóund, and láid in sóme dark róom.
ANTIPHOLUS OF E.	Say, whérefore dídst thou lóck me fórth to-dáy?
ADRIANA	I díd not, géntle húsband, lóck thee fórth.

ANTIPHOLUS OF E.	Dissémbling hárlot, thóu art fálse in áll,
	And árt conféderate wíth a dámnëd páck
	To máke a lóathsome ábject scórn of mé;
	But wíth these náils I'll plúck out thése false éyes
	That wóuld behóld in mé this shámeful spórt.
ADRIANA	O, bínd him, bínd him; lét him nót come néar me.
PINCH	More cómpaný! The fíend is stróng withín him.

[*Enter three or four to bind him*]

LUCIANA	Ay mé, poor mán, how pále and wán he lóoks!
ANTIPHOLUS OF E.	What, wíll you múrder mé?
PINCH	Go bínd this mán, for hé is frántic tóo.

[*They bind Dromio*]

ADRIANA	Good máster Dóctor, sée him sáfe convéy'd
	Hóme to my hóuse. O móst unháppy dáy!

[*Exeunt*]

Scene 6

[*Scene: a street in the city. Enter the Duke of Ephesus and attendants, with Adriana, Luciana, Angelo and citizens*]

ADRIANA

May it pléase your Gráce, Antípholús, my húsband,
Who Í made lórd of mé and áll I hád
At yóur impórtant létters – thís ill dáy
A móst outrágeous fít of mádness tóok him,
That désp'ratelý he húrried thróugh the stréet,
With hím his bóndman áll as mád as hé,
Dóing displéasure tó the cítizéns —

[*Enter a Messenger*]

MESSENGER

O místress, místress, shíft and sáve yoursélf!
My máster ánd his mán are bóth broke lóose,
Béaten the máids a-rów and bóund the dóctor,
Whose béard they háve sing'd óff with bránds of fíre;
And éver, ás it bláz'd, they thréw on hím
Great páils of púddled míre to quénch the háir.
My máster préaches pátience tó him, ánd the whíle
His mán with scíssors nícks him líke a fóol;
And súre, unléss you sénd some présent hélp,
Betwéen them théy will kíll the cónjurér.
Hark, hárk, I héar him, místress; flý, be góne!

DUKE OF E.

Come, stánd by mé; fear nóthing. Gúard with <u>hálberds</u>.   [*weapons*

[*Enter Antipholus of Ephesus, and Dromio of Ephesus*]

ANTIPHOLUS OF E.

Jústice, most grácious Dúke; O gránt me jústice!
Éven for the sérvice thát long sínce I díd thee,
When Í bestríd thee ín the wárs, and tóok
Deep scárs to sáve thy lífe; éven for the blóod
That thén I lóst for thée, now gránt me jústice.
Jústice, sweet Prínce, agáinst that wóman thére!
Shé whom thou gáv'st to mé to bé my wífe,
That háth abúsëd ánd dishónoured mé
Éven in the stréngth and héight of ínjurý.
Beyónd imáginátion ís the wróng
That shé this dáy hath shámeless thrówn on mé.

DUKE OF E.

Discóver hów, and thóu shalt fínd me júst.

ANTIPHOLUS OF E.

This dáy, great Dúke, she shút the dóors upón me,
While shé with hárlots féasted ín my hóuse.

DUKE OF E.

A gríevous fáult. Say, wóman, dídst thou só?

ADRIANA	Nó, my good lórd. Mysélf, hé, and my síster,
	Todáy did díne togéther. Só befáll my sóul
	As thís is fálse he búrdens mé withál!
LUCIANA	Ne'er máy I lóok on dáy nor sléep on níght
	But shé tells tó your Híghness símple trúth!
ANGELO	O pérjur'd wóman! Théy are bóth forswórn.
	In thís the mádman jústly chárgeth thém.
ANTIPHOLUS OF E.	My líege, I ám advísëd whát I sáy;
	Néither distúrbëd wíth the efféct of wíne,
	Nor héady-rásh, provók'd with ráging íre,
	Albéit my wróngs might máke one wíser mád.
	This wóman lóck'd me óut this dáy from dínner;
	But thén, retúrning tó my hóuse, we mét
	My wífe, her síster, ánd a rábble móre
	Of víle conféderátes. Alóng with thém
	They bróught one Pínch, a húngry léan-fac'd víllain,
	A thréadbare júggler, ánd a fórtune-téller,
	A néedy, hóllow-éy'd, sharp-lóoking wrétch,
	A líving déadman. Thís pernícious sláve,
	Forsóoth, took ón him ás a cónjurér,
	And gázing ín mine éyes, féeling my púlse,
	And wíth no fáce, as 'twére, outfácing mé,
	Cries óut I wás posséss'd. Then áll togéther
	They féll upón me, bóund me, bóre me thénce,
	And ín a dárk and dánkish váult at hóme
	There léft me ánd my mán, both bóund togéther;
	Till, gnáwing wíth my téeth my bónds in súnder,
	I gáin'd my fréedom, ánd immédiatelý
	Ran híther tó your Gráce; whom Í beséech
	To gíve me ámple sátisfáctión
	For thése deep shámes and gréat indígnitíes.

[*Enter Antipholus of Syracuse and Dromio of Syracuse. All gather to see them*]

ANTIPHOLUS OF S.	Most míghty Dúke, vouchsáfe me spéak a wórd.
	Is nót your náme, sir, cáll'd Antípholús
	And ís not thát your bóndman Drómió?
ADRIANA	I sée two húsbands, ór mine éyes decéive me.
DROMIO OF S.	Í, sir, am Drómió; commánd him awáy.
DROMIO OF E.	Í, sir, am Drómió; pray lét me stáy.
DUKE OF E.	These twó Antípholús', these twó so líke,
	And thése two Drómios, cánnot bút be bróthers,
	Which áccidéntallý are mét togéther.
	Antípholús, thou cám'st from Córinth fírst?

ANTIPHOLUS OF S.	No, sír, not Í; I cáme from Sýracúse.
DUKE OF E.	Stay, stánd apárt; I knów not whích is whích.
ANTIPHOLUS OF E.	Í came from Córinth, mý most grácious lórd.
DROMIO OF E.	And Í with hím.
ADRIANA	Whích of you twó did díne with mé to-dáy?
ANTIPHOLUS OF S.	Í, gentle místress.
ADRIANA	And áre not yóu my húsband?
ANTIPHOLUS OF E.	No; Í say náy to thát.
ANTIPHOLUS OF S.	And só do Í, yet díd she cáll me só;
	I sée we stíll did méet each óther's mán,
	And Í was tá'en for hím, and hé for mé,
	And théreupón these érrors áre aróse.
ANTIPHOLUS OF E.	Renównëd Dúke, vouchsáfe to táke the páins
	To héar at lárge discóursëd áll our fórtunes.
DUKE OF E.	With áll my héart.

[Exeunt all but the Dromios]

DROMIO OF E.	Methínks you áre my gláss and nót my bróther;
	I sée by yóu I ám a swéet-fac'd yoúth.
	Will yóu walk ín to sée their góssipíng?
DROMIO OF S.	Not Í, sir; you áre my élder.
DROMIO OF E.	That's a question; how shall we try it?
DROMIO OF S.	We'll draw cuts for the senior; till then, lead thou first.
DROMIO OF E.	Nay, then, thus;
	We cáme intó the wórld like bróther and bróther,
	And now lét's go hánd in hánd, not óne befóre anóther.

[Exeunt]

Questions

1. The characters in these scenes are perplexed, angry and grieved. Why then do we laugh? At what moment, if at all, does the action stop being funny?

2. A novelist can describe his or her characters' thoughts to us, but a dramatist has to find other ways of letting us into their minds. What value do the soliloquies have in these scenes?

3. In Scene 2 Dromio of Ephesus describes to Adriana his conversation with the wrong Antipholus. Compare his account with what was actually said in Scene 1. How does Dromio make the encounter more sensational?

4. Show how the characters' choice of 'you' or 'thou' depends on their mood in Scene 3.

5. What have the Dromios in common with other Shakespearean servants you know?

6. 'Ay, ay, Antipholus, look strange and frown . . . ' (Scene 3). How does the patterning of the language in Adriana's speech give it emotional power?

7. Are the Antipholus twins as identical in character as they are in appearance? Describe any distinguishing traits.

8. Remembering that the twins have to be similar in appearance, what kind of costumes do you think would be best for this play? How do you imagine Doctor Pinch should look?

9. If you were staging these scenes, how would you use scenery, lighting and sound to create the mysterious atmosphere of Ephesus?

10. If these scenes are played before an audience, to avoid having a narrator read out the paragraph introducing Scene 5, the action described there could be acted out in dumb-show accompanied by music. Suppose Antipholus of Syracuse fell in love with Luciana; suppose merchants of the city presented their wares to one Antipholus and then demanded payment from the other; suppose Dromio of Ephesus had a sweetheart . . . Write an outline for one such scene.

11. If you were directing a performance, what reactions would you want from the other characters on stage when Antipholus of Syracuse makes his entrance in Scene 6?

12. Have you seen any other comedy where the cause of the confusion is a case of mistaken identity? Write a short story or drama about the confusion caused by twins.

13. How might a story of mistaken identity have a *tragic* outcome?

Part Three

The Wars of the Roses

[from *Henry VI, Parts One, Two and Three* and *Richard III*]

King Henry VI, of the house of Lancaster, grandson to the usurper Bolingbroke, and son to the conqueror King Henry V, inherited from his forebears their titles but nothing of the ruthlessness needed to maintain them.

The ambitious Richard Plantagenet, Duke of York, saw in Henry's vulnerability a chance to put forward his own strong claim to the throne – to take from Lancaster by force what they, by force, had won.

For thirty years in the second half of the fifteenth century England was racked with civil war as the two royal houses – York and Lancaster – battled for the crown.

Scene 1

The Fall of Gloucester

King Henry's one wise councillor, his uncle, Humphrey of Gloucester, is envied and hated by the Queen, Margaret, and by the other lords. The King watches, helpless, as they set about his destruction.

[*Scene: the royal palace in London. Enter the King, the Queen, Cardinal Beaufort, the Dukes of Suffolk, York and Buckingham, and guards*]

KING HENRY I múse my Lórd of Glóucester ís not cóme.
'Tis nót his wónt to bé the híndmost mán,
Whaté'er occásion kéeps him fróm us nów.

QUEEN MARGARET Can yóu not sée, or wíll ye nót obsérve
The stråcngeness óf his álter'd cóuntenánce?
With whát a májestý he béars himsélf;
How ínsolént of láte he ís becóme.
How próud, how péremptory, ånd unlíke himsélf?
We knów the tíme since hé was míld and áffable,

QUEEN MARGARET And íf we díd but glánce a fár-off lóok
(continued) Immédiatelý he wás upón his knée,
That áll the cóurt admír'd him fór submíssion.
But méet him nów and bé it ín the mórn,
When évery óne will gíve the tíme of dáy,
He kníts his brów and shóws an ángry éye
And pásseth bý with stíff unbówëd knée,
Disdáining dúty thát to ús belóngs.

SUFFOLK Well háth your Híghness séen intó this dúke;
And hád I fírst been pút to spéak my mínd,
I thínk I shóuld have tóld your Gráce's tále.
Smooth rúns the wáter whére the bróok is déep,
And ín his símple shów he hárbours tréason.

CARDINAL Díd he not, cóntrarý to fórm of láw,
Devíse strange déaths for smáll offénces dóne?

YORK And díd he nót, in hís protéctorshíp,
Lévy great súms of móney thróugh the réalm
For sóldiers' páy in Fránce, and néver sént it?

BUCKINGHAM Tut, thése are pétty fáults to fáults unknówn
Which tíme will bríng to líght in smóoth Duke Húmphrey.

KING HENRY My lórds, at ónce: the cáre you háve of ús;
To mów down thórns that wóuld annóy our fóot,
Is wórthy práise; but sháll I spéak my cónscience?
Our kínsman Glóucester ís as ínnocént
From méaning tréason tó our róyal pérson
As ís the súcking lámb or hármless dóve:
The Dúke is vírtuous, míld, and tóo well gíven
To dréam on évil ór to wórk my dównfall.

[*Enter Gloucester*]

GLOUCESTER All háppinéss untó my lórd the Kíng!
Párdon, my líege, that Í have stáy'd so lóng.

SUFFOLK Nay, Glóucester, knów that thóu art cóme too sóon,
Unléss thou wért more lóyal thán thou árt.
I dó arrést thee óf high tréason hére.

GLOUCESTER Well, Súffolk, thou shált not sée me blúsh
Nor chánge my cóuntenánce for thís arrést:
A héart unspótted ís not éasily dáunted.
The púrest spríng is nót so frée from múd
As Í am cléar from tréason tó my sóvereign.
Whó can accúse me? Whérein ám I guílty?

Arrangement © Gilian West 1995. Multiple copies may be made by the purchasing institution or individual only.

YORK	'Tis thóught, my lórd, that yóu took bríbes of Fránce
	And, béing Protéctor, stáy'd the sóldiers' páy;
	By méans wheróf his Híghness háth lost Fránce.
GLOUCESTER	Is ít but thóught so? Whát are théy that thínk it?
	I néver róbb'd the sóldiers óf their páy
	Nor éver hád one pénny bríbe from Fránce.
	So hélp me Gód, as Í have wátch'd the níght –
	Ay, níght by níght – in stúdying góod for Éngland!
CARDINAL	It sérves you wéll, my lórd, to sáy so múch.
GLOUCESTER	I sáy no móre than trúth, so hélp me Gód!
YORK	In yóur protéctorshíp you díd devíse
	Strange tórtures fór offénders, néver héard of,
	That Éngland wás defám'd by týranný.
GLOUCESTER	Why, 'tís well knówn that whíles I wás Protéctor
	Píty was áll the fáult that wás in mé;
	For Í should mélt at án offénder's téars,
	And lówly wórds were ránsom fór their fáult.
SUFFOLK	My lórd, these fáults are éasy, quíckly ánswer'd;
	But míghtier crímes are láid untó your chárge,
	Wheróf you cánnot éasily púrge yoursélf.
	I dó arrést you ín his Híghness' náme.
	And hére commít you tó my Lord Cárdinál
	To kéep untíl your fúrther tíme of tríal.
KING HENRY	My Lórd of Glóucester, 'tís my spécial hópe
	That yoú will cléar yoursélf from áll suspénce.
	My cónscience télls me yóu are ínnocént.
GLOUCESTER	Ah, grácious lórd, these dáys are dángeróus!
	I knów their cómplot ís to háve my lífe;
	And íf my déath might máke this ísland háppy
	And próve the périod óf their týranný,
	I wóuld expénd it wíth all wíllingnéss.
	But míne is máde the prólogue tó their pláy;
	For thóusands móre that yét suspéct no péril
	Will nót conclúde their plótted trágedý.
CARDINAL	Sirs, táke awáy the Dúke, and gúard him súre.
GLOUCESTER	Ah, thús King Hénry thróws awáy his crútch
	Befóre his légs be fírm to béar his bódy!
	Thús is the shépherd béaten fróm thy síde,
	And wólves are gnárling whó shall gnáw thee fírst.
	Ah, thát my féar were fálse! ah, thát it wére!
	For, góod King Hénry, thý decáy I féar.

[Exit, guarded]

KING HENRY	My lórds, what tó your wísdom séemeth bést
	Dó or undó, as íf oursélf were hére.
QUEEN MARGARET	Whát, will your Híghness léave the Párliamént?
KING HENRY	Ay, Márgarét; my héart is drówn'd with gríef,
	Whose flóod begíns to flów withín mine éyes;
	Ah, Úncle Húmphrey, ín thy fáce I sée
	The máp of hónour, trúth and lóyaltý!
	And yét, good Húmphrey, ís the hóur to cóme
	That é'er I próv'd thee fálse or féar'd thy fáith.
	What lóuring stár now énvies thý estáte
	That thése great lórds, and Márgarét our Quéen,
	Do séek subvérsion óf thy hármless lífe?
	Thou néver dídst them wróng, nor nó man wróng;
	And ás the bútcher tákes awáy the cálf,
	And bínds the wrétch, and béats it whén it stráys,
	Béaring it tó the blóody sláughter-hóuse,
	Even só, remórseless, háve they bórne him hénce;
	And ás the dám runs lówing úp and dówn,
	Lóoking the wáy her hármless yóung one wént,
	And cán do nóught but wáil her dárling's lóss,
	Even só mysélf bewáils good Glóucester's cáse
	With sád unhélpful téars, and wíth dimm'd éyes
	Look áfter hím, and cánnot dó him góod,
	So míghty áre his vówëd énemíes.
	His fórtunes Í will wéep, and 'twíxt each gróan
	Say 'Whó's a tráitor? Glóucester hé is nóne.'

[Exit]

Scene 2

The Quarrel in the Rose-garden

The Duke of York quarrels with the King's supporters, one of whom, the Duke of Somerset, has been trying to prove that York's father was a traitor.

[Scene: London, a garden near the law-courts. Enter the Earls of Somerset, Suffolk, Warwick and York; Vernon and another Lawyer]

YORK	Great lórds and géntlemén, what méans this sílence?
	Dare nó man ánswer ín a cáse of trúth?
SUFFOLK	Withín the Témple Háll we wére too lóud;
	The gárden hére is móre convéniént.
YORK	Then sáy at ónce if Í maintáin'd the trúth:
	Or élse was wrángling Sómerset ín th'érror?
SUFFOLK	Faith, Í have béen a trúant ín the láw
	And néver yét could fráme my wíll to ít;
	And thérefore fráme the láw untó my wíll.
SOMERSET	Judge yóu, my Lórd of Wárwick, thén, betwéen us.
WARWICK	Betwéen two háwks, which flíes the hígher pítch;
	Betwéen two dógs, which háth the déeper móuth;
	Betwéen two bládes, which béars the bétter témper;
	Betwéen two hórses, whích doth béar him bést;
	Betwéen two gírls, which háth the mérriest éye –
	I háve perháps some shállow spírit of júdgment;
	But ín these níce sharp <u>quíllets</u> óf the láw,
	Good fáith, I ám no wíser thán a <u>dáw</u>.
YORK	Tut, tút, here ís a mánnerlý forbéarance:
	The trúth appéars so náked ón my síde
	That ány púrblind éye may fínd it óut.
SOMERSET	And ón my síde it ís so wéll appárell'd,
	So cléar, so shíning ánd so évidént,
	That ít will glímmer thróugh a blínd man's éye.
YORK	Since yóu are tóngue-tied ánd so lóath to spéak,
	In dúmb significánts procláim your thóughts.
	Let hím that ís a trúe-born géntlemán
	And stánds upón the hónour óf his bírth,
	If hé suppóse that Í have pléaded trúth,
	From óff this bríer plúck a white róse with mé.
SOMERSET	Let hím that ís no cóward nór no flátterer,
	But dáre maintáin the párty óf the trúth,
	Plúck a red róse from óff this thórn with mé.

[*quibbles*

[*jackdaw*

WARWICK	I lóve no cólours; ánd, withóut all cólour
	Of báse insínuáting flátterý,
	I plúck this whíte rose wíth Plantágenét.
SUFFOLK	I plúck this réd rose wíth young Sómersét,
	And sáy withál I thínk he héld the ríght.
VERNON	Stay, lórds and géntlemén, and plúck no móre
	Till yóu conclúde that hé upón whose síde
	The féwest róses áre cropp'd fróm the trée
	Shall yíeld the óther ín the ríght opínion.
SOMERSET	Good Máster Vérnon, ít is wéll objécted;
	If Í have féwest, Í subscríbe in sílence.
YORK	And Í.
VERNON	Then fór the trúth and pláinness óf the cáse,
	I plúck this pále and máiden blóssom hére,
	Gíving my vérdict ón the whíte rose síde.
SOMERSET	Príck not your fínger ás you plúck it óff,
	Lest, bléeding, yóu do páint the whíte rose réd,
	And fáll on mý side só, agáinst your wíll.
VERNON	If Í, my lórd, for mý opínion bléed,
	Opínion sháll be súrgeon tó my húrt
	And kéep me ón the síde where stíll I ám.
SOMERSET	Well, wéll, come ón; who élse?
LAWYER	[*To Somerset*] Unléss my stúdy ánd my bóoks be fálse,
	The árgumént you héld was wróng in yóu;
	In sígn whereóf I plúck a whíte rose tóo.
YORK	Now, Sómersét, whére is your árgumént?
SOMERSET	Hére in my scábbard, méditáting thát
	Shall dýe your whíte rose ín a blóody réd.
YORK	Meantíme your chéeks do cóunterféit our róses;
	For pále they lóok with féar, as wítnessíng
	The trúth on óur side.
SOMERSET	Nó, Plantágenét,
	'Tis nót for féar but ánger thát thy chéeks
	Blúsh for pure sháme to cóunterféit our róses,
	And yét thy tóngue will nót conféss thy érror.
YORK	Hath nót thy róse a cánker, Sómersét?
SOMERSET	Hath nót thy róse a thórn, Plantágenét?
YORK	Ay, shárp and píercing, tó maintáin his trúth;
	Whiles thý consúming cánker éats his fálsehood.
SOMERSET	Well, Í'll find fríends to wéar my bléeding róses,
	That sháll maintáin what Í have sáid is trúe,
	Where fálse Plantágenét dare nót be séen.

YORK   Now, bý this máiden blóssom ín my hánd,
I scórn thee ánd thy fáshion, péevish bóy.
And, bý my sóul, this pále and ángry róse,
As cógnizánce of mý blood-drínking háte,
Will Í for éver, ánd my fáction, wéar,
Untíl it wíther wíth me tó my gráve,
Or flóurish tó the héight of mý degrée.

SUFFOLK   Go fórward, ánd be chók'd with thý ambítion!
And só farewéll untíl I méet thee néxt.

[Exeunt Suffolk and Somerset]

YORK   Hów I am bráv'd, and múst perfórce endúre it!

WARWICK   This blót that théy objéct agáinst your hóuse
Shall bé wip'd óut ín the next Párliamént.
Meantíme, in sígnal óf my lóve to thée,
Will Í upón thy párty wéar this róse;
And hére I próphesý: this bráwl to-dáy,
Grówn to this fáction ín the Témple Gárden,
Shall sénd betwéen the Réd Rose ánd the Whíte
A thóusand sóuls to déath and déadly níght.

[Exeunt]

67

Scene 3

The Death of York

The Duke of York raises an army to force Henry to surrender the crown, but he has reckoned without the ferocious Queen.

[*Scene: a field of battle in Yorkshire. Enter the Duke of York*]

YORK
The ármy óf the Qúeen hath gót the fíeld;
And áll my fóllowers tó the éager fóe
Turn báck and flý, like shíps befóre the wínd.
Ah, hárk! The fátal fóllowers dó pursúe,
And Í am fáint and cánnot flý their fúry;
The sánds are númb'red thát make úp my lífe;
Hére must I stáy, and hére my lífe must énd.

[*Enter Queen Margaret, Lord Clifford, the Earl of Northumberland, and Soldiers*]

NORTHUMBERLAND Yíeld to our mércy, próud Plantágenét.

CLIFFORD
Áy, to such mércy ás his rúthless árm
With dównright páyment shów'd untó my fáther.

YORK
My áshes, ás the phóenix, máy bring fórth
A bírd that wíll revénge upón you áll.
And ín that hópe I thrów mine éyes to héaven,
Scórning whaté'er you cán afflíct me wíth.
Why cóme you nót? What! múltitúdes and féar?

NORTHUMBERLAND What wóuld your Gráce have dóne untó him nów?

QUEEN MARGARET Brave wárriors, Clífford ánd Northúmberlánd,
Come, máke him stánd upón this mólehill hére
That <u>ráught</u> at móuntains wíth outstrétchëd árms.   [*reached*
Whát, was it yóu that wóuld be Éngland's kíng?
Was't yóu that révell'd ín our párliamént
And máde a préachment óf your hígh descént?
Whére are your <u>méss</u> of sóns to báck you nów?   [*set of four*
The wánton Édward ánd the lústy Géorge?
And whére's that váliant cróok-back pródigý,
Dícky your bóy, that wíth his grúmbling vóice
Was wónt to chéer his dád in mútiníes?
Or, wíth the rést, whére is your dárling Rútland?
Look, Yórk: I stáin'd this nápkin wíth the blóod
That váliant Clífford wíth his rápier's póint
Made íssue fróm the bósom óf the bóy;
And íf thine éyes can wáter fór his déath,
I gíve thee thís to drý thy chéeks withál.
Alás, poor Yórk! but thát I háte thee déadly,
I shóuld lamént thy míseráble státe.
I príthee gríeve to máke me mérry, Yórk.
What, háth thy fíery héart so párch'd thine éntrails
That nót a téar can fáll for Rútland's déath?
Why árt thou pátient, mán? Thou shóuldst be mád;
And Í to máke thee mád do móck thee thús.
Stamp, ráve, and frét, that Í may síng and dánce.
Thou woúldst be fée'd, I sée, to máke me spórt;
Yórk cannot spéak unléss he wéar a crówn.
A crówn for Yórk! – and, lórds, bow lów to hím.
Hóld you his hánds whilst Í do sét it ón.

[*Putting a paper crown on his head*]

Ay, márry, sír, now lóoks he líke a kíng!
Óff with the crówn and wíth the crówn his héad;
And, whílst we bréathe, take tíme to dó him déad.

YORK O tíger's héart wrápp'd in a wóman's híde!
How cóuldst thou dráin the lífe-blood óf the chíld,
To bíd the fáther wípe his éyes withál,
And yét be séen to béar a wóman's fáce?
Wómen are sóft, mild, pítifúl, and fléxible:
Thou stérn, obdúrate, flínty, róugh, remórseless.
Bíd'st thou me ráge? Why, nów thou hást thy wísh;
Wouldst háve me wéep? Why, nów thou hást thy wíll;
For ráging wínd blows úp incéssant shówers,
And whén the ráge alláys, the ráin begíns.
These téars are mý sweet Rútland's óbsequíes;
And évery dróp cries véngeance fór his déath
'Gainst thée, fell Clífford, and thée, false Frénchwomán.
There, táke the crówn, and wíth the crówn my cúrse;
And ín thy néed such cómfort cóme to thée
As nów I réap at thý too crúel hánd!
Hard-héarted Clífford, táke me fróm the wórld;
My sóul to héaven, my blóod upón your héads!

NORTHUMBERLAND Had hé been sláughter-mán to áll my kín,
I shóuld not fór my lífe but wéep with hím,
To sée how ínly sórrow grípes his sóul;

QUEEN MARGARET What, wéeping-rípe, my lórd Northúmberlánd?
Thínk but upón the wróng he díd us áll,
And thát will quíckly drý thy mélting téars.

CLIFFORD Hére's for my óath, hére's for my fáther's déath.

[*Stabbing him*]

QUEEN MARGARET And hére's to ríght our géntle-héarted kíng.

[*Stabbing him*]

YORK Ópen Thy gátes of mércy, grácious Gód!
My sóul flies thróugh these wóunds to séek out Thée.

[*Dies*]

QUEEN MARGARET Óff with his héad, and sét it ón York gátes;
That Yórk may óverlóok the tówn of Yórk.

[*Exeunt*]

Scene 4

Father and Son

After the death of York, his sons continue the fight for the crown. King Henry watches the battle raging in the distance.

[*Scene: near a field of battle. Enter King Henry*]

KING HENRY

This báttle fáres líke to the mórning's wár,
When dýing clóuds conténd with grówing líght,
What tíme the shépherd, blówing óf his náils,
Can néither cáll it pérfect dáy nor níght.
Now swáys it thís way, líke a míghty séa
Fórc'd by the tíde to cómbat wíth the wínd;
Now swáys it thát way, líke the sélfsame séa
Fórc'd to retíre by fúry óf the wínd.
Hére on this mólehill wíll I sít me dówn.
To whóm God wíll, thére be the víctorý!
For Márgarét my quéen, and Clífford tóo,
Have chíd me fróm the báttle, swéaring bóth
They prósper bést of áll when Í am thénce.
Wóuld I were déad, if Gód's good wíll were só!
For whát is ín this wórld but gríef and wóe?

[*Enter a Son, bearing the body of his Father*]

SON

Ill blóws the wínd that prófits nóbodý.
This mán whom hánd to hánd I sléw in fíght
May bé posséssëd wíth some stóre of crówns;
And Í, that háply táke them fróm him nów,
May yét ere níght yield bóth my lífe and thém
To sóme man élse, as thís dead mán doth mé.
Who's thís? O Gód! It ís my fáther's fáce,
Whóm in this cónflict Í unwáres have kíll'd.
O héavy tímes, begétting súch evénts!
From Lóndon bý the Kíng was Í press'd fórth;
My fáther, béing the Éarl of Wárwick's mán,
Cáme on the párt of Yórk, préss'd by his máster;
And Í, who át his hánds recéiv'd my lífe,
Have bý my hánds of lífe beréavëd hím.
Párdon me, Gód, I knéw not whát I díd.
And párdon, fáther, fór I knéw not thée.
My téars shall wípe awáy these blóody márks;
And nó more wórds till théy have flów'd their fíll.

KING HENRY   O píteous spéctaclé! O blóody tímes!
Whiles líons wár and báttle fór their déns,
Poor hármless lámbs abíde their énmitý.
Wéep, wretched mán; I'll áid thee téar for téar;
And lét our héarts and éyes, like cívil wár,
Be blínd with téars and bréak o'erchárg'd with gríef.

[*Enter a Father, bearing the body of his Son*]

FATHER   Thóu that so stóutly háth resísted mé,
Gíve me thy góld, if thóu hast ány góld;
For Í have bóught it wíth an húndred blóws.
But lét me sée. Is thís our fóeman's fáce?
Ah, nó, no, nó, it ís mine ónly són!
Ah, bóy, if ány lífe be léft in thée,
Thrów up thine éye! See, sée what shów'rs aríse,
Blówn with the wíndy témpest óf my héart
Upón thy wóunds, that kílls mine éye and héart!
O, píty, Gód, this míseráble áge!
What strátagéms, how féll, how bútcherlý,
Erróneous, mútinous, ánd unnáturál,
This déadly quárrel dáily dóth begét!
O bóy, thy fáther gáve thee lífe too sóon,
And háth beréft thee óf thy lífe too láte!

KING HENRY   Wóe above wóe! gríef more than cómmon gríef!
O thát my déath would stáy these rúthful déeds!
O píty, píty, géntle héaven, píty!
The réd rose ánd the whíte are ón his fáce,
The fátal cólours óf our stríving hóuses:
Wíther one róse, and lét the óther flóurish!
If yóu conténd, a thóusand líves must pérish.

SON   Hów will my móther fór a fáther's déath
Take ón with mé, and né'er be sátisfíed!

FATHER   Hów will my wífe for sláughter óf my són
Shed séas of téars, and né'er be sátisfíed!

KING HENRY   How wíll the cóuntry fór these wóeful chánces
Misthínk the Kíng, and nót be sátisfíed!

SON   Was éver són so rúed a fáther's déath?

FATHER   Was éver fáther só bemóan'd his són?

KING HENRY   Was éver kíng so gríev'd for súbjects' wóe?
Múch is your sórrow; míne ten tímes so múch.

SON   I'll béar thee hénce, where Í may wéep my fíll.

[*Exit, with the body*]

FATHER   These árms of míne shall bé thy wínding-shéet;
                         My héart, sweet bóy, shall bé thy sépulchré,
                         For fróm my héart thine ímage né'er shall gó;
                         My síghing bréast shall bé thy fúneral béll;
                         I'll béar thee hénce; and lét them fíght that wíll,
                         For Í have múrdered whére I shóuld not kíll.

                                                  [*Exit, with the body*]

KING HENRY   Sad-héarted mén, much óvergóne with cáre,
                         Here síts a kíng more wóeful thán you áre.

Scene 5

The Death of the Prince of Wales

At the Battle of Tewkesbury the Queen's army is finally defeated. York's eldest son has already declared himself King as Edward IV.

	[*Scene: the battle-field, after the fighting has ceased. Enter King Edward, his two brothers, George, now Duke of Clarence, and Richard, now Duke of Gloucester, and Soldiers, with Queen Margaret and her son, Edward, Prince of Wales, as prisoners*]
KING EDWARD	Bring fórth the gállant; lét us héar him spéak. Édward, what sátisfáction cánst thou máke For béaring árms, for stírring úp my súbjects, And áll the tróuble thóu hast túrn'd me tó?
PRINCE OF WALES	Spéak like a súbject, próud ambítious Yórk. Suppóse that Í am nów my fáther's móuth; Resígn thy cháir, and whére I stánd kneel thóu, Whilst Í propóse the sélf-same wórds to thée Which, tráitor, thóu wouldst háve me ánswer tó.
GLOUCESTER	By héaven, brát, I'll plágue ye fór that wórd.
QUEEN MARGARET	Ay, thóu wast bórn to bé a plágue to mén.
GLOUCESTER	For Gód's sake, táke awáy this cáptive scóld.
PRINCE OF WALES	Nay, táke awáy this scólding cróokback ráther.
KING EDWARD	Péace, wilful bóy, or Í will chárm your tóngue.
PRINCE OF WALES	I knów my dúty; yóu are áll undútifúl. Lascívious Édward, ánd thou pérjur'd Géorge, And thóu misshápen Díck, I téll ye áll Í am your bétter, tráitors ás ye áre; And thóu usúrp'st my fáther's ríght and míne.
KING EDWARD	Take thát, the líkeness óf this ráiler hére.
	[*Stabs him*]
GLOUCESTER	Spráwl'st thou? Take thát, to énd thy ágoný.
	[*Stabs him*]
CLARENCE	And thére's for twítting mé with pérjurý.
	[*Stabs him*]
QUEEN MARGARET	O, kíll me tóo!
GLOUCESTER	Márry, and sháll.
KING EDWARD	Hold, Ríchard, hóld; for wé have dóne too múch.
GLOUCESTER	Why shóuld she líve to fíll the wórld with wórds?
KING EDWARD	Whát, doth she swóon? Use méans for hér recóvery.

GLOUCESTER Clárence, excúse me tó the Kíng my bróther.
 I'll hénce to Lóndon ón a sérious mátter;
 Ére ye come thére, be súre to héar some néws.
CLARENCE What? what?
GLOUCESTER The Tower! the Tower!

                  [*Exit*]

QUEEN MARGARET O Néd, sweet Néd, spéak to thy móther, bóy!
 Cánst thou not spéak? O tráitors! múrderérs!
 Théy that stabb'd Cáesar shéd no blóod at áll,
 Did nót offénd, nor wére not wórthy bláme,
 If thís foul déed were bý to équal ít.
 He wás a mán: thís, in respéct, a chíld;
 And mén ne'er spénd their fúry ón a chíld.
 What's wórse than múrderér, that Í may náme it?
 No, nó, my héart will búrst, an íf I spéak –
 And Í will spéak, that só my héart may búrst.
 Bútchers and víllains! blóody cánnibáls!
 How swéet a plánt have yóu untímely crópp'd!
 You háve no chíldren, bútchers; íf you hád,
 The thóught of thém would háve stirr'd úp remórse.
 But íf you éver chánce to háve a chíld,
 Lóok in his yóuth to háve him só cut óff
 As, déathsmen, yóu have ríd this swéet young prínce!
KING EDWARD Awáy with hér; go béar her hénce perfórce.

      [*Exit Queen Margaret, led out forcibly*]

 Where's Ríchard góne?
CLARENCE To Lóndon, áll in póst; and, ás I guéss,
 To máke a blóody súpper ín the Tówer.
KING EDWARD He's súdden, íf a thíng comes ín his héad.
 Now márch we hénce. Dischárge the cómmon sórt
 With páy and thánks; and lét's awáy to Lóndon
 And sée our géntle quéen how wéll she fáres.
 By thís, I hópe, she háth a són for mé.

               [*Exeunt*]

Scene 6

The Death of Henry VI

Richard of Gloucester has determined that the crown shall be his. As yet there are several lives barring his way: one by one they must be removed. The Prince of Wales has been dispatched, but King Henry still lives.

[*Scene: a room in the Tower of London. Enter King Henry, and to him, Richard*]

GLOUCESTER	Good dáy, my lórd. Whát, at your bóok so hárd?
KING HENRY	Áy, my good lórd – my lórd, I shóuld say ráther.
	'Tis sín to flátter; 'góod' was líttle bétter.
	'Good Glóucester' ánd 'good dévil' wére alíke.
	And bóth prepósterous; thérefore, nót 'good lórd'.
	But whérefore dóst thou cóme? Is't fór my lífe?
GLOUCESTER	Think'st thóu I ám an éxecútionér?
KING HENRY	A pérsecútor Í am súre thou árt.
	If múrdering ínnocénts be éxecúting,
	Why, thén thou árt an éxecútionér.
	And thús I próphesý, that mány a thóusand

[*part

	Which nów mistrúst no <u>párcel</u> óf my féar,
	And mány an óld man's sígh, and mány a wídow's,
	And mány an órphan's wáter-stánding éye –
	Mén for their sóns, wíves for their húsbands,
	Órphans fór their párents' tímeless déath –
	Shall rúe the hóur that éver thóu wast bórn.
	The ówl shríek'd at thy bírth – an évil sígn;
	The níght-crow críed, abóding lúckless tíme;
	Dogs hówl'd, and hídeous témpest shóok down trées;
	The ráven róok'd her ón the chímney tóp,

	And cháttering <u>píes</u> in dísmal díscords súng;

[*magpies

	Thy móther félt móre than a móther's páin,
	And yét brought fórth léss than a móther's hópe.
	To wít, an índigést defórmëd lúmp,
	Not líke the frúit of súch a góodly trée.
	Téeth hadst thou ín thy héad when thóu wast bórn,
	To sígnifý thou cám'st to bíte the wórld;
	And íf the rést be trúe which Í have héard,
	Thou cám'st –
GLOUCESTER	I'll héar no móre. Díe, prophet, ín thy spéech.

[*Stabs him*]

For thís, amóngst the rést, was Í ordáin'd.

KING HENRY

Áy, and for múch more sláughter áfter thís.
O, Gód forgíve my síns and párdon thée!

[*Dies*]

GLOUCESTER

Whát, will the aspíring blóod of Láncastér
Sínk in the gróund? I thóught it wóuld have móunted.
Sée how my swórd wéeps for the póor King's déath.
O, máy such púrple téars be álways shéd
From thóse that wísh the dównfall óf our hóuse!
If ány spárk of lífe be yét remáining,
Down, dówn to héll; and sáy I sént thee thíther –

[*Stabs him again*]

Í, that have néither píty, lóve, nor féar.
Indéed, 'tis trúe that Hénry tóld me óf;
For Í have óften héard my móther sáy
I cáme intó the wórld with mý legs fórward.
Had Í not réason, thínk ye, tó make háste
And séek their rúin thát usúrp'd our ríght?
The mídwife wónder'd; ánd the wómen críed
'O, Jésus bléss us, hé is bórn with téeth!'
And só I wás, which pláinly sígnifíed
That Í should snárl, and bíte, and pláy the dóg.
Then, sínce the héavens have sháp'd my bódy só,
Let héll make cróok'd my mínd to ánswer ít.
I háve no bróther, Í am líke no bróther;
And thís word 'lóve', which gréybeards cáll divíne,
Be residént in mén líke one anóther,
And nót in mé! I ám mysélf alóne.
Clárence, bewáre; thou kéep'st me fróm the líght,
But Í will sórt a pítchy dáy for thée;
King Hénry ánd the Prínce his són are góne.
Clárence, thy túrn is néxt, and thén the rést;
Cóunting mysélf but bád till Í be bést.
I'll thrów thy bódy ín anóther róom,
And tríumph, Hénry, ín thy dáy of dóom.

[*Exit, with the body*]

Scene 7

The Death of Clarence

King Edward, convinced by Richard that their brother is a traitor, sends Clarence to the Tower.

[*Scene: a room in the Tower. Clarence, asleep. Enter the Keeper, and to him, two Murderers*]

KEEPER	What wóuldst thou, féllow, ánd how cám'st thou híther?
1ST MURDERER	I would speak with Clarence, and I came hither on my legs.
KEEPER	What, so brief?
2ND MURDERER	'Tis better, sir, than to be tedious. Let him see our commission and talk no more.

[*Keeper reads it*]

KEEPER	I ám, in thís, commánded tó delíver
	The nóble Dúke of Clárence tó your hánds.
	I wíll not réason whát is méant herebý,
	Becáuse I wíll be guíltless fróm the méaning.
	There líes the Dúke asléep; ánd there bé the kéys.
	I'll tó the Kíng and sígnifý to hím
	That thús I háve resígn'd to yóu my chárge.
1ST MURDERER	You may, sir; 'tis a point of wisdom. Fare you well.

[*Exit Keeper*]

2ND MURDERER	What, shall I stab him as he sleeps?
1ST MURDERER	No; he'll say 'twas done cowardly, when he wakes.
2ND MURDERER	Why, he shall never wake until the great judgment-day.
1ST MURDERER	Why, then he'll say we stabb'd him sleeping.
2ND MURDERER	The urging of that word judgment hath bred a kind of remorse in me.
1ST MURDERER	What, art thou afraid?
2ND MURDERER	Not to kill him, having a warrant; but to be damn'd for killing him, from the which no warrant can defend me.
1ST MURDERER	I thought thou hadst been resolute.
2ND MURDERER	So I am, to let him live.
1ST MURDERER	I'll back to the Duke of Gloucester and tell him so.
2ND MURDERER	Nay, I prithee, stay a little. I hope this passionate humour of mine will change; it was wont to hold me but while one tells twenty.
1ST MURDERER	How dost thou feel thyself now?
2ND MURDERER	Faith, some certain dregs of conscience are yet within me.
1ST MURDERER	Remember our reward, when the deed's done.
2ND MURDERER	<u>Zounds</u>, he dies; I had forgot the reward. [*an oath*
1ST MURDERER	Where's thy conscience now?
2ND MURDERER	O, in the Duke of Gloucester's purse. Come, shall we fall to work?

1ST MURDERER	Take him on the <u>costard</u> with the hilts of thy sword, and then *[head*
	chop him in the <u>malmsey-butt</u> in the next room. *[wine barrel*
2ND MURDERER	O excellent device! and make a sop of him.
1ST MURDERER	Soft! he wakes.
2ND MURDERER	Strike!
1ST MURDERER	No, we'll reason with him.
CLARENCE	Where art thou, Keeper? Give me a cup of wine.
2ND MURDERER	You shall have wine enough, my lord, anon.
CLARENCE	In Gód's name, whát art thóu?
	Who sént you híther? Whérefore dó you cóme?
2ND MURDERER	To, to, to —
CLARENCE	To múrder mé?
BOTH	Ay, ay.
CLARENCE	You scárcely háve the héarts to téll me só,
	And thérefore cánnot háve the héarts to dó it.
	Whereín, my friends, have Í offénded yóu?
	Are yóu drawn fórth amóng a wórld of mén
	To sláy the ínnocent? Whát is mý offénce?
	Whére is the évidénce that dóth accúse me?
	I chárge you, ás you hópe to háve redémption
	By Chríst's dear blóod shéd for our gríevous síns,
	That yóu depárt and láy no hánds on mé.
	The déed you úndertáke is dámnablé.
1ST MURDERER	Whát we will dó, we dó upón commánd.
CLARENCE	If yóu are hír'd for <u>méed</u>, go báck agáin, *[payment*
	And Í will sénd you tó my bróther Glóucester,
	Who sháll rewárd you bétter fór my lífe
	Than ány wíll for tídings óf my déath.
2ND MURDERER	You áre decéiv'd: your bróther Glóucester hátes you.
CLARENCE	O, dó not slánder hím, for hé is kínd.
1ST MURDERER	Ríght, as snów in hárvest. Come, yóu decéive yoursélf:
	'Tis hé that sénds us tó destróy you hére.
2ND MURDERER	Look behind you, my lord.
1ST MURDERER	[*Stabs him*]
	Take thát, and thát. If áll this wíll not dó,
	I'll drówn you ín the málmsey-bútt withín.

                      [*Exit with the body*]

2ND MURDERER	A blóody déed, and désperatelý dispátch'd!
	How fáin, like Pílate, wóuld I wásh my hánds
	Of thís most gríevous múrder!

                      [*Exit*]

Scene 8

The Lord Protector

When Edward IV dies, only his two little sons, Edward V and Richard of York, are keeping Richard of Gloucester, now the Lord Protector, from the crown.

[*Scene: a street in London. Enter the young King Edward V, attended by Richard of Gloucester, the Duke of Buckingham and other Lords*]

KING EDWARD	Sáy, uncle Glóucester, íf our bróther cóme,
	Whére shall we sójourn tíll our córonátion?
GLOUCESTER	Whére it seems bést untó your róyal sélf.
	If Í may cóunsel yóu, some dáy or twó
	Your Híghness sháll repóse you át the Tówer.
KING EDWARD	I dó not líke the Tówer, of ány pláce.
	Did Július Cáesar búild that pláce, my lórd?
GLOUCESTER	He díd, my grácious lórd, begín that pláce,
	Which, sínce, succéeding áges háve reédifíed.
	[*Aside*] So wíse so yóung, they sáy, do néver live lóng.
KING EDWARD	That Július Cáesar wás a fámous mán.
	Déath makes no cónquest óf this cónquerór;
	For nów he líves in fáme, though nót in lífe.
	I'll téll you whát, my cóusin Búckinghám –
BUCKINGHAM	Whát, my grácious lórd?
KING EDWARD	An íf I líve untíl I bé a mán,
	I'll wín our áncient ríght in Fránce agáin,
	Or díe a sóldier ás I lív'd a kíng.
GLOUCESTER	[*Aside*] Short súmmers líghtly háve a fórward spríng.

[*Enter Richard of York, with attendants*]

BUCKINGHAM	Nów, in good tíme, here cómes the Dúke of Yórk.
KING EDWARD	Ríchard of Yórk, how fáres our lóving bróther?
YORK	Wéll, my dread lórd; so múst I cáll you nów.
KING EDWARD	Áy brother, tó our gríef, as ít is yóurs.
GLOUCESTER	How fáres our cóusin, nóble Lórd of Yórk?
YORK	I thánk you, géntle úncle. Ó, my lórd,
	You sáid that ídle wéeds are fást in grówth.
	The Kíng my bróther háth outgrówn me fár.
GLOUCESTER	He háth, my lórd.
YORK	And thérefore ís he ídle?
GLOUCESTER	Ó, my fair cóusin, Í must nót say só.
YORK	Then hé is móre behólding to yóu than Í.
GLOUCESTER	He máy commánd me ás my sóveréign;
	But yóu have pówer in mé as ín a kínsman.

YORK	I práy you, úncle, gíve me this dágger.
GLOUCESTER	My dágger, líttle cóusin? With áll my héart!
	My lórd, will't pléase you páss alóng?
	Mysélf and mý good cóusin Búckinghám
	Will tó your móther, tó entréat of hér
	To méet you át the Tówer and wélcome yóu.
YORK	Whát, will you gó untó the Tówer, my lórd?
KING EDWARD	My Lórd Protéctor néeds will háve it só.
YORK	I sháll not sléep in quíet át the Tówer.
GLOUCESTER	Whý, whát should you féar?
YORK	Márry, my úncle Clárence's ángry ghóst.
	My grándam tóld me hé was múrder'd thére.
KING EDWARD	I féar no úncles déad.
GLOUCESTER	Nor nóne that líve, I hópe.
KING EDWARD	An íf they líve, I hópe I néed not féar.
	But cóme, my lórd; wíth a héavy héart,
	Thínking on thém, go Í untó the Tówer.

[*Exeunt*]

Scene 9

The Weeping Queen

Richard of Gloucester seizes the crown and has his two young nephews murdered in the Tower. Queen Elizabeth, Edward IV's widow, with the old Duchess of York, their grandmother, laments the death of her little sons. They are joined by Queen Margaret, who since the death of her husband has haunted the Court, half-crazed.

[Scene: the royal palace in London. Enter Queen Elizabeth, the old Duchess of York, and, behind, Queen Margaret]

QUEEN ELIZABETH Áh, my poor prínces! áh, my ténder bábes!
My únblown flówers, néw-appéaring swéets!
If yét your géntle sóuls flý in the áir
And bé not fíx'd in dóom perpétuál,
Hóver abóut me with your áiry wíngs
And héar your móther's lámentátión.

DUCHESS So mány míseriés have cráz'd my vóice
That mý woe-wéaried tóngue is stíll and múte.

QUEEN ELIZABETH Ah, whó hath ány cáuse to móurn but wé?

QUEEN MARGARET *[Coming forward]* If sórrow cán admít socíetý,
Tell ó'er your wóes agáin by víewing míne.
I hád an Édward, tíll a Ríchard kíll'd him;
I hád a húsband, tíll a Ríchard kíll'd him;
Thou hádst an Édward, tíll a Ríchard kíll'd him;
Thou hádst a Ríchard, tíll a Ríchard kíll'd him.

DUCHESS I hád a Ríchard tóo, and thóu didst kíll him;
I hád a Rútland tóo, thou hólp'st to kíll him.

QUEEN MARGARET Thou hádst a Clárence tóo, and Ríchard kíll'd him.

DUCHESS O Hárry's wífe, tríumph not ín my wóes!
God wítness with me, Í have wépt for thíne.

QUEEN MARGARET Bear wíth me; Í am húngry fór revénge,
And nów I clóy me with behólding ít.
Thy Édward hé is déad, that kíll'd my Édward;
The óther Édward déad, to quít my Édward;
Thy Clárence hé is déad that stább'd my Édward.
Ríchard yet líves, hell's bláck intélligéncer.
But at hánd, at hánd,
Ensúes his píteous ánd unpítied énd.
Earth gápes, hell búrns, fiends róar, saints práy,
To háve him súddenlý convéy'd from hénce.
Cáncel his bónd of lífe, dear Gód, I práy,
That Í may líve and sáy 'The dóg is déad'.

QUEEN ELIZABETH O, thóu didst próphesý the tíme would cóme
That Í should wísh for thée to hélp me cúrse
That bóttled spíder, thát foul búnch-back'd tóad.

QUEEN MARGARET I cáll'd thee thén vain flóurish óf my fórtune;
I cáll'd thee thén poor shádow, páinted quéen,
One héav'd a-hígh to bé hurl'd dówn belów,
A móther ónly móck'd with twó fair bábes,
A quéen in jést, ónly to fíll the scéne.
Whére is thy húsband nów? Whére be thy bróthers?
Whére be thy twó sons? Whérein dóst thou jóy?
Who súes, and knéels, and sáys 'God sáve the Quéen'?
Whére be the bénding péers that fláttered thée?
Whére be the thrónging tróops that fóllowed thée?
Declíne all thís, and sée what nów thou árt:
For háppy wífe, a móst distréssëd wídow;
For jóyful móther, óne that wáils the náme;
For óne being sú'd to, óne that húmbly súes;
For Quéen, a véry cáitiff crówn'd with cáre;   [*wretched creature*
For shé that scórn'd at mé, now scórn'd of mé;
For shé being féar'd of áll, now féaring óne;
For shé commánding áll, obéy'd of nóne.
Thus háth the cóurse of jústice whírl'd abóut
And léft thee bút a véry préy to tíme,
Háving no móre but thóught of whát thou wást
To tórture thée the móre, being whát thou árt.
Thou dídst usúrp my pláce, and dóst thou nót
Usúrp the júst propórtion óf my sórrow?
Nów thy proud néck bears hálf my búrden'd yóke,
From whích even hére I slíp my wéary héad
And léave the búrden óf it áll on thée.
Farewéll, York's wífe, and quéen of sád mischánce;
These Énglish wóes shall máke me smíle in Fránce.

[*Exit*]

Scene 10

Bosworth

(i)

The Duke of Richmond, an heir of the house of Lancaster, leads an army to invade England and overthrow the tyrant. At Bosworth in Leicestershire, he meets with King Richard's army.

[Scene: the camps of the two armies, the night before battle. Enter to his tent King Richard, with Ratcliff, one of his men]

KING RICHARD Bíd my guard wátch; léave me.
Rátcliff, abóut the míd of níght cóme to my tént
And hélp to árm me. Léave me, I sáy.

[Exit Ratcliff. Richard sleeps]

[Enter to his tent Richmond, with followers]

RICHMOND Once móre, good níght, kind lórds and géntlemén.

[Exeunt all but Richmond]

O Thóu, whose cáptain Í accóunt mysélf,
Lóok on my fórces wíth a grácious éye;
Pút in their hánds Thy brúising írons of wráth,
That théy may crúsh down wíth a héavy fáll
The usúrping hélmets óf our ádversáries!
Make ús Thy mínistérs of chástisemént,
That wé may práise Thee ín the víctorý!
To theé I dó comménd my wátchful sóul
Ere Í let fáll the wíndows óf mine éyes.
Sléeping and wáking, Ó, defénd me stíll! *[Sleeps]*

[Enter the Ghost of the young Edward, Prince of Wales, son to Henry VI]

PRINCE *[To Richard]* Let mé sit héavy ón thy sóul tomórrow!
Think hów thou stább'st me ín my príme of yóuth
At Téwkesburý; despáir, therefóre, and díe!
[To Richmond] Be chéerful, Ríchmond; fór the wróngëd sóuls
Of bútcher'd prínces fíght in thý behálf.
King Hénry's íssue, Ríchmond, cómforts thée.

[Enter the Ghost of Henry VI]

KING HENRY

[To Richard]　When Í was mórtal, mý anóinted bódy
By thée was púnchëd fúll of déadly hóles.
Thínk on the Tówer and mé. Despáir, and díe.
Hárry the Síxth bids thée despáir and díe.
[To Richmond]　Vírtuous and hóly, bé thou cónquerór!
Hárry, that próphesíed thou shóuldst be Kíng,
Doth cómfort thée in thy sléep. Líve and flóurish!

[Enter the Ghosts of the two young Princes, sons to Edward IV]

PRINCES

[To Richard]　Dréam on thy cóusins smóthered ín the Tówer.
Let ús be léad withín thy bósom, Ríchard,
And wéigh thee dówn to rúin, sháme, and déath!
Thy néphews' sóuls bid thée despáir and díe.
[To Richmond]　Sléep, Richmond, sléep in péace, and wáke in jóy;
Good ángels gúard thee fróm the <u>bóar's</u> annóy!　*[a boar was
Richard's heraldic badge*

Líve, and begét a háppy ráce of kíngs!
Édward's unháppy sóns do bíd thee flóurish.

[The Ghosts vanish. King Richard starts out of his dream]

KING RICHARD

Gíve me anóther hórse. Bínd up my wóunds.
Have mércy, Jésu! Sóft! I díd but dréam.
O cóward cónscience, hów dost thóu afflíct me!
The líghts burn blúe. It ís now déad midníght.
Cold féarful dróps stánd on my trémbling flésh.
Whát do I féar? Mysélf? There's nóne else bý.
Ríchard loves Ríchard; thát is, Í am Í.
Is thére a múrderer hére? No – yés, I ám.
My cónscience háth a thóusand séveral tóngues,
And évery tóngue brings ín a séveral tále,
And évery tále condémns me fór a víllain.
Pérjury, pérjury, ín the hígh'st degrée;
Múrder, stern múrder, ín the dír'st degrée;
All séveral síns, all ús'd in éach degrée,
Thróng to the bár, crýing all 'Gúilty! gúilty!'
I sháll despáir. There ís no créature lóves me;
And íf I díe no sóul will píty mé:
And whérefore shóuld they, sínce that Í mysélf
Fínd in mysélf no píty tó mysélf?
Methóught the sóuls of áll that Í had múrder'd
Cáme to my tént, and évery óne did thréat
Tomórrow's véngeance ón the héad of Ríchard.

[*Enter Ratcliff*]

RATCLIFF	My lórd!
KING RICHARD	Zóunds, who is thére?
RATCLIFF	Rátcliff, my lórd; 'tis Í. The éarly víllage-cóck
	Hath twíce done sálutátion tó the mórn;
	Your fríends are úp and búckle ón their ármour.
KING RICHARD	O Rátcliff, Í have dréam'd a féarful dréam!
	What thínk'st thou – wíll our friends próve all trúe?
RATCLIFF	No dóubt, my lórd.
KING RICHARD	O Rátcliff, I féar, I feár.
RATCLIFF	Náy, good my lórd, be nót afráid of shádows.
KING RICHARD	Bý the apóstle Pául, shádows toníght
	Have strúck more térror tó the sóul of Ríchard
	Than cán the súbstance óf ten thóusand sóldiers
	Ármëd in próof and léd by shállow Ríchmond.
	'Tís not yét near dáy. Come, gó with mé;
	Únder our ténts I'll pláy the éaves-droppér,
	To sée if ány méan to shrínk from mé.

[*Exeunt*]

[*Enter Lords to Richmond's tent*]

LORDS	Good mórrow, Ríchmond!
	How háve you slépt, my lórd?
RICHMOND	The swéetest sléep and fáirest-bóding dréams
	That éver ént'red ín a drówsy héad
	Have Í since yóur depárture hád, my lórds.
	Methóught their sóuls whose bódies Ríchard múrder'd
	Cáme to my tént and críed on víctorý.
	I prómise yóu my sóul is véry jócund
	Ín the remémbrance óf so fáir a dréam.
	How fár intó the mórning ís it, lórds?
LORDS	Upón the stróke of fóur.
RICHMOND	Whý, then 'tis tíme to árm and gíve diréction.

[*Exeunt*]

(ii)

[Scene: the field of battle. Enter the Duke of Norfolk and Soldiers. To him, one of King Richard's men, Catesby]

CATESBY
Réscue, my Lórd of Nórfolk, réscue, réscue!
The Kíng enácts more wónders thán a mán,
Dáring an ópposíte to évery dánger.
His hórse is sláin, and áll on fóot he fíghts,
Séeking for Ríchmond ín the thróat of déath.
Réscue, fair lórd, or élse the dáy is lóst.

[Enter King Richard]

KING RICHARD
A hórse! a hórse! my kíngdom fór a hórse!

CATESBY
Withdráw, my lórd; I'll hélp you tó a hórse.

KING RICHARD
Sláve, I have sét my lífe upón a <u>cást</u>   *[a throw of the dice*
And Í will stánd the házard óf the díe.
I thínk there bé six Ríchmonds ín the fíeld;
Fíve have I sláin to-dáy instéad of hím.
A hórse! a hórse! my kíngdom fór a hórse!

[Exeunt]

(iii)

[Scene: another part of the field. Enter King Richard and Richmond; they fight; Richard is slain. Enter the Earl of Derby with other lords and soldiers]

RICHMOND
Gód and your árms be práis'd, victórious fríends;
The dáy is óurs, the blóody dóg is déad.

DERBY
Courágeous Ríchmond, wéll hast thóu acquít thee!
Lo, hére, this lóng-usúrpëd róyaltý
Fróm the dead témples óf this blóody wrétch
Have Í pluck'd óff, to gráce thy bróws withál.
Wéar it, enjóy it, ánd make múch of ít.

RICHMOND
Great Gód of héaven, sáy Amén to áll!
What mén of náme are sláin on éither síde?

DERBY
Jóhn, Duke of Nórfolk, Wálter, Lórd Ferrérs,
Sir Róbert Brákenbury, ánd Sir Wílliam Brándon.

RICHMOND   Intér their bódies ás becómes their bírths.
Procláim a párdon tó the sóldiers fléd
That ín submíssion wíll retúrn to ús.
And thén, as wé have tá'en the sácramént,
We wíll uníte the whíte rose ánd the réd.
Smíle heaven upón this fáir conjúnctión,
That lóng have frówn'd upón their énmitý!
What tráitor héars me, ánd says nót amén?
Éngland hath lóng been mád, and scárr'd hersélf;
The bróther blíndly shéd the bróther's blóod,
The fáther ráshly sláughter'd hís own són,
The són, compéll'd, been bútcher tó the síre;
All thís divíded Yórk and Láncastér.
O, nów let Ríchmond ánd Elízabéth,
The trúe succéeders óf each róyal hóuse,
By Gód's fair órdinánce conjóin togéther!
And lét their héirs, God, íf Thy wíll be só,
Enrích the tíme to cóme with smóoth-fac'd péace,
With smíling plénty, ánd fair prósperous dáys!
Abáte the édge of tráitors, grácious Lórd,
That wóuld redúce these blóody dáys agaín
And máke poor Éngland wéep in stréams of blóod!
Lét them not líve to táste this lánd's incréase
That wóuld with tréason wóund this fáir land's péace!
Now cívil wóunds are stópp'd, péace lives agáin –
That shé may lóng live hére, God sáy amén!*

                                                      [*Exeunt*]

NOTE

*Richmond married Edward IV's surviving child, his daughter Elizabeth, and became King as Henry VII – the first Tudor.

Questions

1. Note all the curses, prophecies and omens you can find in these ten scenes and trace how they are fulfilled. How might the staging of this drama (lighting, music, etc.) intensify our sense of the supernatural at work in the action?
2. *Scene 1: The Fall of Gloucester*. Write a speech for a lawyer defending Gloucester against the charge of treason and summing up his case.
3. *Scene 2: The Quarrel in the Rose-garden*. How does Shakespeare make this scene frightening?
4. *Scene 3: The Death of York*. 'The sands are numb'red that make up my life.' Explain York's meaning in this line.
5. *Scene 4: Father and Son*. This scene does not advance the plot. Why does Shakespeare include it?
6. *Scene 5: The Death of the Prince of Wales*. 'Men ne'er spend their fury on a child.' What has Margaret forgotten?
7. *Scene 6: The Death of Henry VI*. What do the King's last words tell us about his character?
8. *Scene 7: The Death of Clarence*. From the evidence of this scene, when do you think Shakespeare feels it is necessary to use verse?
9. *Scene 8: The Lord Protector*. Why is it impossible to laugh at the jokes in this scene?
10. *Scene 9: The Weeping Queen*. Demonstrate how Shakespeare uses rhetorical patterns of language and rhetorical questions to emphasize the ironies that mock the two Queens.
11. *Scene 10: Bosworth*. Imagine how you would stage the fight between Richard and Richmond. Would they both fight courageously? Would they both fight chivalrously?
12. Which speeches do you find the most powerful? Is there anything special about the use of language in these speeches? How do metaphor, simile and rhetorical patterning increase the emotional effect?
13. List the different ways in which the characters *justify* their killing of other people. Do you find some justifications more acceptable than others? Why?
14. 'No soul will pity me.' How much pity do you feel for Richard?
15. Which would you argue is the most beautiful line in all the ten scenes? Which is the most ironic?
16. If you were staging this play, how would you use costume to help identify characters and their loyalties?
17. Find a recent newspaper story of a *battle for power* (not necessarily political power), somewhere in the world. Could you turn this story into a play? Think about the following:

    Do the characters have emotions and motives that an audience could identify with?

    Does the story build up to an exciting climax?

    How many scenes would the play need and what information would each scene have to contribute?

    What effect should each scene have on the audience, and what effect should the whole play have?

    Have you enough people in your group to write one scene each?

    Who is going to direct the performance?